A History of Courtship

For Gary
'*My heart, pierced thro' with fierce delight,*
Bursts into blossom in his sight.'

(From *Fatima* by Alfred, Lord Tennyson)

A History of Courtship

800 Years of Seduction

Tania O'Donnell

Skyhorse Publishing

Library of Congress Cataloging-in-Publication Data is available on file.

Cover design by Dominic Allen

Print ISBN: 978-1-5107-0858-7
Ebook ISBN: 978-1-5107-0870-9

Printed in the United States of America

Contents

Conclusion
Happiness in relationships relies on many factors but a few good sense bits of advice from our ancestors is not to be sniffed at – a summary of the best of their advice.

Acknowledgments

I'd like to thank: my father, the novelist Hamraz Ahsan, for convincing me to write for a living; Jen Newby, formerly at Pen & Sword Books, for commissioning this book, for her superb editing skills and meticulous improvements to the manuscript; Dominic Allen for his beautiful book jacket design; Eloise, Heather, Lisa and all at Pen & Sword books for their patience, kindness, and hard work; Chelsey Fox for the loan of a wonderfully inspiring book; Emily Brand for her excellent History of Love blog (http://historyofloveblog.wordpress.com); Meg Schultz for the use of her photo and her family's incredible story (http://hpugh.blogspot.co.uk), my family – both the Ahsans and the O'Donnells (specific mentions for Pawan, Munazza, Welshon Bull, Mum Farah, Mum Vie and Neen Phups) – for their unstinting support; Poorna Bell for giving me a HuffpostUK blog in which to express my opinions on relationships; Raj Kaushal for many long conversations about love; the glorious children in my life – Katie, Zachary, Hassan, Sara, and Leela West – for selflessly spreading happiness wherever they go; and Bunty for the late night cognacs and cigars.

I'd also like to thank the staff at the London Library and the British Library for their kindness in dealing with a nervous and skittish library user. But, above all, I must thank Gary for courting me so well that I pledged my troth.

Introduction

All courtship is the art of convincing the other person of your innate desirability. However, our ideas of what qualities are desirable have changed over time. In general, assets such as wealth, attractive physical features, and readiness to give tokens of love and admiration remain unchanged. Yet, our ideas about the level of wealth we can marry into, good looks we can acquire through cosmetic means, and, most tellingly, the tokens of love we exchange have dramatically altered.

Our modern notions of love and romance mean that today many Britons find it distasteful to openly consider class or position when choosing a life partner, but in times past assessing a prospective partner's income would have been seen as a perfectly normal, indeed wise, preoccupation.

Many historians date our contemporary ideas about romantic love to the twelfth century and the medieval chivalric code of courtly love. In fact, the idea of finding your 'other half' pre-dates this significantly. Aristophanes (c. 446–c. 386 BCE), a Greek playwright known for his comedic works, is said in Plato's *The Symposium* to have posited that all human beings were originally of three types: male, female, and androgynous. These early humans, according to Aristophanes, had doubled bodies joined at the back. They wheeled around in quite a comical fashion, but were powerful enough to challenge the gods so Zeus split them in two, thereby halving their power while ensuring there were still humans around to worship the gods. Aristophanes uses this creation myth to explain the concept of feeling 'whole' when we meet our 'other halves'.

If the notion of one special person being your true soulmate has been around since the ancient Greeks, we can assume that the idea of romantic love is far older than the early Middle Ages, even if the poetic language of love was not widely recorded in the West before that time.

Whether or not we believe that there were romantic Neanderthals, the consensus is that courtly love codified the angst-ridden, teenage version of 'Falling In Love' writ large, and so the twelfth century is a good place to begin a history of courtship. This is when the idea of tragic love or thwarted love gained strength, with the famous story of Tristan and Isolde. The highest expression of love in the literature and culture of this period is the 'impossible love', and the wooing rather than the winning becomes the most elaborate part of mating rituals.

So if the emotional rollercoaster of the twelfth century is where we start, why end with the traditionally strait-laced nineteenth century? By the twentieth century, globalisation and advances in the speed of travel had changed many of the traditions of courting forever. People were no longer forced to choose a mate from their immediate environs or even social circle. Also it is only in the twentieth century that the notion of established time begins to hold sway in the western world. Being late for an assignation might be considered a terrible faux pas for the modern lover, but given that standard time didn't come into law in the UK until 1880 when the Statues (Definition of Time) Act came into force or in the United States until 1918, when the Standard Time Act was passed by Congress, earlier courting couples might meet at dawn or sunset or at the end of a day's work. This was irrevocably changed as the world became tethered to time.

Among the many bleak aspects of the First World War was the low numbers of eligible men left in the UK after the conflict, leading to a disparity between the sexes and what the papers described as the 'surplus two million' women. Virginia Nicholson writes, in *Singled Out: How Two Million Women Survived Without Men after the First World War* (Penguin, 2007): 'it is beyond doubt that the war had a seismic effect on marital behaviour ... all contemporary accounts take the man shortage for granted, and that many women themselves perceived the courtship arena as a competitive battleground, where defeat was perdition.'

Courtship rituals during this century of upheaval had to change, emboldening women and taking some of the pressure off men. The much-fêted 'birth of the teenager' in 1950s America also changed the rules of courtship for young people. So, as the twentieth century is too unwieldy to include in a concise history of courtship, we end our journey in the nineteenth, when Victorian values still held sway and love still had to seep through social restrictions and propriety.

It is a source of some sadness that near-universal literacy in Britain is a modern notion. We have extremely few written historical sources for those with limited access to education in centuries past – generally speaking, the rural and urban poor. So while men of letters have written extensively about their views of the other social classes they encountered, it is rare indeed to find a written account from a working class individual. Country sayings, folklore, oral histories and family histories can provide some insight into the lives of ordinary people. On the subject of courtship, small superstitions have been recorded not in literature, but passed down through the generations in rhymes and songs – even graffiti inscribed in churches. We can begin to build a picture of the romances of servants and labourers through those snippets of information.

The written evidence we have for courting through the ages comes from the letters of the nobility or the diktats of the Church (an institution that interfered to such a great extent in private lives that one could argue that the Church inadvertently gave birth to romantic love). Then there is the sharply observant literature of Regency authors, such as Jane Austen, to give us a very complete picture of the social lives of the upper classes. And so, in dribs and drabs, scandals and rumours, letters and bawdy tales, we begin to build up a picture of love through the ages.

Does this information have any relevance for the modern lover, beyond humour or the enjoyment of quirky ideas from times past? I believe it does, in that when we examine the history of how couples came together in the past, we begin to appreciate the freedoms we now have. Perhaps we become more grateful that we are no longer forced to marry from the narrow pool of our places of birth or within the rigid confines of status and rank.

When the history of courtship is laid before us, we can celebrate how far we've come in gaining greater equality of the sexes and creating happier marriages – while still remaining watchful for throwbacks to more unenlightened times.

Tania O'Donnell, London,
Summer 2016.

Chapter One

Love at First, Second, or Third Sight

Making new acquaintances and signalling your interest

L et's blame the ancient Greeks for it. The notion that we should fall madly in love at first sight can probably be attributed to all those Greek myths featuring Eros and his arrows of love; the idea being that within the most romantic of love stories you should be 'struck' by an instant flash of passion. However, this doesn't leave much room for getting to know one another before 'falling in love'. And what of childhood sweethearts who have known each other since birth? Is their love or passion in some way diminished because they didn't get the opportunity to meet each other's eyes across a room and declare themselves instantly smitten?

It is easy to forget how far the technological advances of the last century have opened up the world to us, especially in terms of love and romance. Before the Victorian railway boom, the time and expense involved in travelling even relatively short distances meant that most people stayed close to home, choosing a mate from among their acquaintances and family friends. While the upper echelons may have moved around more, even the relationships they formed were constrained by the circles they moved in.

The best a poor village girl in the pre-industrial age could hope for by way of a glamorous stranger was a travelling craftsman looking for work. But this did not stop the idle speculation of youth, and a young maid might turn to childhood rhymes and superstitions in the hope of divining her fate.

The famous 'Tinker, Tailor, Soldier, Sailor' rhyme has its origins in the fifteenth century and was used to predict whom the questioner would marry. The words 'Tinker, Tailor, Soldier, Sailor, Rich Man, Poor Man, Beggar Man, Thief' were chanted as cherry stones or petals on a daisy were counted out. Further verses revealed when you'd marry, your position in married life, what you'd wear on your wedding day, how you'd obtain this clothing, how you'd get to church, and even where you

This 1906 photographic print by E.W. Kelley shows a young woman playing the 'he loves me, he loves me not' game with daisy petals, while a man watches with amusement in the bushes behind her. (*Library of Congress*)

might live afterwards. This provided a harmless diversion to while away a summer afternoon.

Summer is also when the cuckoo's call would be heard. According to an old tradition the number of consecutive cuckoo calls you hear equates to the number of years until you will marry. These 'fateful' signs could be one way of predicting a positive future, but the more enterprising took matters into their own hands and engaged in activities to push

This photographic print from the late nineteenth century is entitled 'Waiting For Him' and depicts a young lady waiting for a gentleman caller. (*Boston Public Library*)

forward contact with their true love. Tucking an ivy leaf into your bosom ensured that the next man who spoke to you would be your beloved – or so tradition dictated. If while shelling peas, you found a pod with nine perfectly shaped peas inside, it was believed to be a sign of good luck. According to superstition, if an unmarried girl should hang the empty pod over the lintel of the front door, the first man to cross the threshold would be her future husband.

These homely superstitions exhibit a longing to know when and whom it would be a girl's destiny to marry. The fact that their intended is expected to appear imminently suggests that most people were aware that they would not marry exotic strangers, but someone with whom they already came into daily contact.

The Victorian explorer Sir Samuel White Baker, for example, at the tender age of twenty-two, chose as his wife, Henrietta, his childhood playmate and the daughter of the local rector, while his brother John picked her sister, Elizabeth. Samuel provides an excellent example of both idealised manners in which we think of love blossoming: childhood sweethearts and the big romantic 'love at first sight'. Henrietta was a childhood companion who later became a loving wife and the mother of his children. However, after her untimely death, Samuel quite remarkably diverged from the usual course of courting within upper class circles and married Florence Barbara Maria, a Hungarian refugee whom he had *bought* in a slave market on the Danube.

Michael Brander writing in his biography of the great hunter and explorer, *The Perfect Victorian Hero*, says that while stranded in Widdin awaiting the go-ahead for a hunting expedition in 1858, Samuel visited a local slave market. There 'Sam saw this beautiful young Hungarian girl, who, on the death or marriage of her erstwhile nurse, had fallen into unscrupulous hands'. She was put up for sale and he outbid all the wealthy Turkish merchants at the auction, bought her, and subsequently married her. It seems strange that Samuel's more sedate, predictable courtship happened when he was in the first flush of youth, while the wild, exotic romance occurred much later in his life.

Yet, this exceptional Victorian case was not the way most British people met a prospective love interest in the past. Even if a young person was in a position to come into contact with strangers, they could not simply wander up to them and engage them in conversation. Or at least those deemed to be ladies and gentlemen could not do so.

In the Regency era, a strict etiquette codified how one was to make a new acquaintance among gentlefolk. Until one had been introduced to an unknown person, it was not considered proper to begin a conversation with them. Upon entry to a new neighbourhood a family could expect to have their neighbours, or more exactly the heads of the local households, call upon them to allow an acquaintance to be formed.

Kidnapping a bride

Many of these rules can be traced back to the historic function of marriage as a contract for increasing wealth. Marriages between members of the monied classes have always been seen as a way to increase one's position in society, either through acquiring advantageous connections or property. In such cases, protecting the maidenheads of womenfolk was supremely, in fact economically, vital.

Historically heiresses could be kidnapped, forced to marry under threat of rape, and sold off to the highest bidder by guardians. A high profile kidnapping occurred on 2 of September 1487, when Robert Bellingham, a nobleman who found favour with King Henry VII for having thwarted one of the pretenders to his throne, nevertheless annoyed the sovereign by abducting the wealthy heiress Margery Beaufitz. Her father had not favoured Bellingham's proposal of marriage, and so the would-be suitor with a band of accomplices broke into the family's home and carried Margery away. Bellingham was imprisoned for flouting the law that Henry had passed against the abduction of women earlier that same year. However, a few months later the case was dropped when an agreement was reached between Bellingham and Margery's father. The couple subsequently married and Bellingham once again found himself in the King's good books.

'An Act Against Taking Away of Women Against Their Will' of 1487 was not some great feminist measure against violence toward women. In fact it was put in place to ensure that the Crown did not lose the revenues

Charles Brandon, Duke of Suffolk, scandalously married his ward in order to get her estate for himself. (*Portrait by Jan Gossaert, c.1516, Public Domain*)

it gained through the orphaned wealthy heirs of their tenants. For any child in such a situation was automatically a ward of the monarch, who could decide to pass on that wardship to a favoured courtier or sell it to a guardian wishing to invest in the hope of future profit.

Charles Brandon, the 1st Duke of Suffolk, chose not to wait for future dividends from his wards and made a bit of a habit of trying to marry them himself. He had to annul the first marriage contract he entered into with a ward when a better wife came along. Elizabeth Grey, an orphaned viscountess, was ditched in favour of Mary Tudor, the sister of Henry VIII. When Mary died in June 1533, Brandon then married his fourteen-year-old ward, Catherine Willoughby, Baroness Willoughby of Eresby. She had been betrothed to his son, but the boy was too young to marry and Brandon did not want to risk losing her substantial estate through a lengthy engagement in a time of high mortality.

Heiress kidnapping was still a problem over a century later, as shown by the case of Elizabeth Malet, granddaughter of Lord Hawley. On 26 May 1665, the 2nd Earl of Rochester, John Wilmot, lived up to his reputation as a libertine and kidnapped the wealthy Elizabeth after she had turned down his proposal of marriage.

Here is Samuel Pepys's diary entry on the matter:

'Thence to my Lady Sandwich's, where, to my shame, I had not been a great while before. Here, upon my telling her a story of my Lord Rochester's running away on Friday night last with Mrs. Mallett, the great beauty and fortune of the North, who had supped at White Hall with Mrs. Stewart, and was going home to her lodgings with her grandfather, my Lord Haly, by coach; and was at Charing Cross seized on by both horse and foot men, and forcibly taken from him, and put into a coach with six horses, and two women provided to receive her, and carried away. Upon immediate pursuit, my Lord of Rochester (for whom the King had spoke to the lady often, but with no successe) was taken at Uxbridge; but the lady is not yet heard of, and the King mighty angry, and the Lord sent to the Tower. Hereupon my Lady did confess to me, as a great secret, her being concerned in this story. For if this match breaks between my Lord Rochester and her, then, by the consent of all her friends, my Lord Hinchingbroke stands fair, and is invited for her. She is worth, and will be at her mother's death (who keeps but a little from her), 2500*l.* per annum.'

Samuel Pepys kept a diary that recorded many of the scandals and trysts of seventeenth century London, as well as his own lascivious behaviour. (*Wellcome Collection*)

The chivalry Lord Rochester showed in having two ladies to receive the kidnapped lady must have sat well with Elizabeth as she later agreed to marry him against her father's wishes.

Scandal and Elopements

Nevertheless there were occasions when such extreme measures to initiate 'love' simply didn't need to be taken. Much to the chagrin of the Church, if you did not have any wealth or land to worry about, you could quite easily get betrothed and move in together with your beloved, without any outside interference. This was shockingly libertarian in the eyes of the clergy, who saw marriage as a sacrament and were keen to reduce the prevalence of 'sin', aka sex outside marriage. There was also the biblical diktat of 'let no man put asunder' what God has joined together.

Annoyingly for the Church, if the correct vows of fidelity and marriage were made between a couple of marriageable age (over the age of fifteen for a 'man' and over twelve for a 'woman'), their marriage was deemed to have been legally binding, with or without the consent of their parents or the presence of clergy. In the words of historian George Gordon Coulton, 'In Chaucer's time, the whole world was a vaster and more commodious Gretna Green.'

Strangely enough, the binding nature of private vows made the Church an unlikely ally in some love stories. The Paston Letters, private documents that span three generations of the Paston family of Norfolk from the fifteenth to the early sixteenth centuries, give a juicy insight into a case in which the Church upheld an informal marriage. The daughter of the family, Margery Paston, fell in love with her father's bailiff, Richard Calle. They secretly married in 1469, angering her parents who set the matter before the bishop. Upon enquiring of the young couple how they had entered into the married state, the clergyman could find no fault with the union and so it stood. The family attempted to dismiss Calle from his post, but his knowledge of their finances and his ability to secure funds from their tenants meant they had to reinstate him.

Brandoin pinx.   *Caldwall sculp.*

A LADIES MAID PURCHASING A LEEK.

Servants might meet a beau in the course of their daily duties, which is why many mistresses banned a maid from having followers. (*This 1772 print entitled A Lady's Maid Purchasing A Leek is by James Caldwall, Library of Congress*)

This case shows that love will thrive wherever there is opportunity. One method of attempting to thwart undesirable matches was to do away with any chance young people had of privacy. Medieval noble women had retainers and ladies-in-waiting to ensure that they were always chaperoned. (The efficacy of chaperons will be described in more detail within Chapter Five.)

By comparison couples from the working classes and the rural poor had a tremendous amount of freedom, with many seeking out their privacy in the lanes and woods outside a cramped communal home. When huge fortunes weren't at stake, it also occasionally made sense to have sex before marriage to 'test' the bride's fertility and many couples tied the knot with the proof of the groom's virility clear for all to see. There were also rural traditions around the seasonal calendar and Pagan hangovers such as May Day celebrations that allowed men and women to freely mix and often resulted in pairings, even if they failed to get these unions legally consummated.

However, on occasion a lack of propriety could lead to a marriage, with the approval of the couple's parents. The practice of 'bundling' which was frowned upon in later, more puritanical years, was deemed a sensible way of allowing couples to get to know each other before marriage. They would spend a night together, fully clothed, sometimes tied down with a board placed down the middle of the bed, in order to talk without having sex. This was practised in seventeenth century Wales and made its way over to eighteenth century New England.

Another example of parental advocacy of impropriety is the most likely apocryphal tale of how Margaret, daughter of the Renaissance statesman Sir Thomas More, was introduced to her husband William Roper. It is related by seventeenth century historian John Aubrey in his collection of biographies, *Aubrey's Brief Lives* (1697). Apparently Roper was led into the bedroom where More's two daughters were asleep, lying naked on a truckle bed. More threw back their covers and the protesting girls turned onto their stomachs to cover their private parts. Roper, having

This print published in *Once A Week* magazine in 1864 shows a courting couple enjoying the relative freedom of a rural romance. (*Public Domain*)

charmingly said that he had now seen both sides, gave Margaret's buttock a pat with his walking stick to indicate his choice. As Aubrey puts it 'here was all the trouble of the wooing'. If this is a true story, one can only hope it was an unusual one.

Another lascivious old man was the famed diarist Samuel Pepys, who would miss no opportunity to force his advances on long-suffering chambermaids and even strangers sitting next to him in the pew at a church. Here is a typical entry from his diary, dated 18 August 1667:

'I walked towards White Hall, but, being wearied, turned into St. Dunstan's Church, where I heard an able sermon of the minister of the place; and stood by a pretty, modest maid, whom I did labour to take by the hand and the body; but she would not, but got further and further from me; and, at last, I could perceive her to take pins out of her pocket to prick me if I should touch her again – which seeing I did forbear, and was glad I did spy her design. And then I fell to gaze upon another pretty maid in a pew close to me, and she on me; and I did go about to take her by the hand, which she suffered a little and then withdrew. So the sermon ended, and the church broke up, and my amours ended also, and so took coach and home …'

Dancing and romancing

As many commentators have said on the matter, in earlier times with more contracted marriages, courtship often began after a marriage instead of before. Perhaps the reason we find the arranged marriage customs of Eastern cultures so alien is that they have largely died out within our own culture. Our modern ways of meeting a beau do, however, have one precedent in history – that of the dance.

While today it is occasionally possible to meet a prospective beau in a bar or nightclub, dances in assembly rooms were once the only sanctioned opportunity for young people to meet and flirt under the watchful eye of guardians and chaperons. Even if attending a dance or ball did not secure a match, it was deemed a good place to practice one's social skills and to show off one's allurements.

An account from the diarist Katherine Plymley on 3 December 1796, describes the glamour – and also clamour – of a ball in Bath. Quite apart from the drama of a ballroom lit up by more dazzling light than would be normal of an evening, the participants also created quite the spectacle.

'I met Lady Glynne at Mrs. Falconers public day & went with her to the ball. Miss Charlotte & Miss Williams joined us, the latter however became discomposed because we declined pushing thro' the crowd (for such it was, 12 hundred persons being present) from the ball room to the tea room & left us for a more congenial party. The Prince & Duke came early to the ball room with the Dutchess.... The Dutchess I thought rather a pretty little woman, but quite over rouged, so were all the ladies of her party, the Prince extremely good humour'd & pleasant, I do not like the Duke's countenance. They were both dressed in plain blue with the star. The Dutchess's body & train was white spotted with gold, trimmed round the neck & down the sides with narrow black velvet studded with diamonds, her head dress a turban, diamond crescent, & large plume of feathers, diamond necklace & earings.'

One of the most famous literary love stories – that of Elizabeth Bennet and Fitzwilliam Darcy in Jane Austen's *Pride and Prejudice* (1813) – begins at an assembly room ball. This tempestuous relationship starts off with Darcy snubbing Lizzy by refusing to ask her to dance. With a scarcity of partners at the dance, Elizabeth is obliged to sit out some dances and Darcy's more amiable friend, Bingley, takes a break from his own partners to try and convince him to be more agreeable and ask Lizzy to dance. He responds: "She is tolerable; but not handsome enough to tempt me; I am in no humour at present to give consequence to young ladies who are slighted by other men. You had better return to your partner and enjoy her smiles, for you are wasting your time with me."

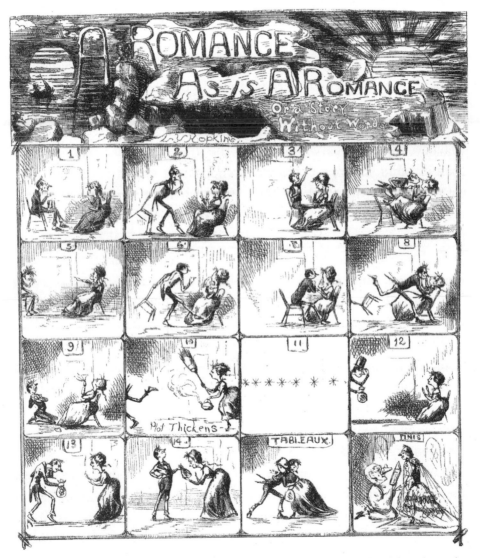

A satirical picture story published in the late nineteenth century paper *Wild Oats* shows the importance of wealth in having one's affections returned. (*Public Domain*)

For Darcy to stand out dances when partners are few was a distinct insult to not just Elizabeth but all the ladies present who were unable to dance due to a lack of willing gentlemen.

Provincial assemblies such as the one depicted at Meryton were held monthly in the winter season, often coinciding with a full moon to naturally light the path of carriages coming to the dance. It was the ideal opportunity to meet neighbours and make new acquaintances, especially if you were new to the area. The master of ceremonies, or an otherwise acquainted person, could introduce you to the local dignitaries and the flirting could begin in a respectable manner.

Interestingly, you didn't have to be rich to enjoy a dance. Henry Mayhew, the Victorian chronicler of the lives of the poor and working class in London, wrote of 'twopenny-hops' that were often attended by costermongers, men and women who sold fruit, vegetables and fish in the street from barrows. For a two pence entry fee, dancers could take part in jigs, country dances, and polkas. Mayhew places the attendance at these dances to be between thirty to one hundred of both sexes, although women were slightly more predominant. Their ages varied between fourteen and forty-five and the dancing was of the 'vigorous, laborious' kind.

'There is sometimes a good deal of drinking,' reveals Mayhew, 'some of the young girls being often pressed to drink, and frequently yielding to the temptation.' The chivalrous costermonger men would treat the women to drinks at these events, possibly in the hope that libation might serve as an introduction to a young lady in the absence of the master of ceremonies at grander affairs.

Having managed through fate or fortune, chance or dance, to make a suitable acquaintance with someone you wished to marry, without the aid of social media, how could you then signal your interest?

Signalling interest

The Renaissance author, Count Baldassare Catiglione, wrote in the *Book of the Courtier* (1528) about the power of the lover's gaze; 'Those lively spirits that issue out at the eyes because they are engendered nigh the heart, entering in like case into the eyes that they are levelled at, like a shaft to the prick, naturally pierce the heart'. To this day, our most effective flirting technique is the furtive glance held a tad too long. The huge benefit of a simple stare to show your willingness to get to know someone better is that it is not hampered by the constraints of social niceties. You can stare discreetly at anyone and then look away quickly if you're caught at it.

The natural blushes that occur in such a situation are also said to be a great enhancement to a woman's looks. Walter Houghton, writing in his guide *American Etiquette and Rules of Politeness* (1883), advises that gentlemen shouldn't allow a flirtatious glance to veer into odd or impolite behaviour. 'Avoid looking full into the faces of strangers whom you meet, especially of ladies.'

An article by Richard Steele in *The Spectator* that was printed in 1711 references a letter that the journalist claimed was from a lady called 'Celimene' who complained of being encumbered with a young relation from the country who was sent up to her for education and was not genteel enough to know the ways of society. Described as having 'no way to express herself but by her tongue and that always to signify her meaning… she means nothing by walking but to change her place', the unsophisticated young countrywoman was not aware of the powerful arsenal of glances and movement that were at her disposal. Steele's correspondent wondered how such a girl was to be tutored.

Steele's response was to despair of the manner in which the younger generation were being educated. 'In our daughters we take care of their persons and neglect their minds; in our sons we are so intent upon adorning their minds that we wholly neglect their bodies. It is from this that you shall see a young lady celebrated and admired in all the assemblies about town, when her elder brother is afraid to come into a room.' He describes how upon growing old enough to no longer need her nursemaid, a girl is handed over to a dancing master for instruction on how to be charming. '... And with a collar round her neck the pretty wild thing is taught a fantastical gravity of behaviour, and forced to a particular way of holding her head, heaving her breast and moving with her whole body; and all this under pain of never having a husband, if she steps, looks or moves awry. This gives the young lady wonderful workings of the imagination, what is to pass between her and this husband that she is every moment told of ... Thus her fancy is engaged to turn all her endeavours to the ornament of her person ... from this general folly of parents we owe our present numerous race of coquets.'

While Steele may have been scathing about the 'coquetry' of tutored women, by Victorian times women everywhere were continuing to use subtle glances to indicate romantic interest. In using her eyes as her weapon of choice, a young Victorian lady could even make use of the more boring parts of attending church on a Sunday to cast an eye over the congregation for suitable earthly distractions. While her spiritual scorecard might have suffered from such carnal thoughts, her dance card would have filled up rather quickly.

Could props such as fans also be employed to indicate a lady's interest in a gentleman? Stories of the language of fans being used in the seventeenth and eighteenth centuries abound, but there is little evidence of women using the fan in such a way in the literature of the time. The first guide to using fans for secret communication was published in 1826 by Duvelleroy, a Parisian fan maker, who included a booklet with the fans he sold. This was almost certainly a marketing ploy aimed at gullible young ladies, especially since the gentlemen they were aiming to communicate with were unlikely to have been privy to the intricate meaning of a fan carried in the left hand in front of the face ('I wish to be acquainted'), much less that of twirling it in the right hand ('I love another').

The whole business seems to be the equivalent of young women who read astrological love signs in the hope of arcane knowledge. This is not to say that fans were of no use in courtship, as we will find out in the next chapter. In centuries past it was generally the duty of the man to make the first move. A woman who was interested in a man only had to make herself as alluring as possible and to polish up her accomplishments for occasions when an introduction might happen. For a lady, being generally acknowledged as accomplished was one way of gaining introduction to the right sort of men. By the Regency era, to be considered accomplished you had to have some form of musical aptitude, display intricate sewing skills, be a good conversationalist, and a dainty dancer. It was just as well that there was plenty of time during which affluent women could practise and improve those skills. Victorian debutante Alice Miles wrote in her diary in 1868, aged 17, that 'I consider it every girl's duty to marry £80,000 a year'. This was a clear-eyed statement of why so much time was spent on becoming accomplished. Alice was quite open about the importance of financials in securing a good marriage:

'Sir Samuel has tried to inveigle me into a flirtation, but as I had previously ascertained he has only £4,000 a year … there would be no interested side in any proceedings and he is not sufficiently good looking to render interesting, and a flirtation devoid of either of these indispensible elements does not at all enter into my plan of action.'

Thankfully not all courtships were quite so openly mercenary, as this sweet Victorian example in Jennifer Newby's book *Women's Lives* (2011) shows: 'In 1872, 20-year-old Emily Jowitt from Leeds wrote excitedly to a friend that when she found herself alone with Squire Dearman Birchall on the way back from church, 'just as we were going down the carriage drive, he proposed … the suddenness of it all took my breath away'. While engaged, Emily remarked that she and Dearman 'generally spooned a good deal and said "Oh my darling I do love you so".'

For those not as daring as Squire Dearman, there was no shortage of help to induce a nervous man to make a suitable young woman an offer of marriage. The relations of an eligible man were always on the lookout for a suitable wife, while the relations of an eligible woman were equally keen to get her married off. Of course the opinions of two sets of relations did not always tally and many a coupling was derailed by the ideas and ambitions of those around the young couple.

Chapter Two

Beauty & Seductive Items of Clothing

Arm yourself with these handy historical beautifying and dressing ideas

Historically, there has been a pernicious belief that the two assets a woman should possess when looking for a husband are beauty and wealth. One without the other might still secure a husband, but the absence of both could be a very trying obstacle to marriage for those wanting to wed.

A late fifteenth century illustration of pride from *An illustrated Yorkshire Carthusian Religious Miscellany*. Pride is represented in the form of a young fashionably dressed man attracting the attention of two devils. (*British Library*)

However, men and women throughout the ages have found ways to improve on what God gave them, thereby heartily annoying the Church. Anatole France said, 'Christianity has done much for love by making it a sin.' This was also the case with beauty. With Vanity (more commonly referred to as Pride) depicted as the greatest of the seven deadly sins, the religious establishment was not keen on people tinkering with what God had deemed perfection. While women took the brunt of the anti-beautifying edicts, men were not immune to having their impulses to improve upon nature curbed as well.

Prior to 1615, when Sir Robert Mansell acquired the first patent for the manufacture of 'looking glasses', the wealthy would use polished obsidian to admire (or bemoan) their looks. The Church naturally had something to say about this contemplative gazing; too much gazing into a mirror would make the devil appear. The invention of modern mirrors using silvered glass in 1835 meant mirrors were mass produced and far more widely available. With access to these shiny new instruments in which to gaze, young women were clearly not listening to stuffy decrees at church. Instead, they embraced superstitions, hoping to see an image of their future husbands in the mirror, while brushing their hair and eating an apple. A less terrifying folk belief was that if a man and woman first set eyes upon each other in a mirror, they would make happy spouses.

Even before Venetians learned to silver glass and produce mirrors in the sixteenth century, men and women were concerned with their looks and chose elaborate, and sometimes painful, methods to beautify themselves. The medieval obsession with a high forehead had women plucking their hairlines almost to the top of their heads.

Art and even religious iconography from this time depicts women with large oval faces, plucked eyebrows and high foreheads. Geoffrey De La Tour Landry, writing in 1371, had no sympathy for the pain involved in hair removal and warned that any woman indulging in such vanity would find herself despatched to Hell. There a devil would plunge a burning

This satirical cartoon printed in *Puck* magazine in 1910 shows a woman more in love with her reflection than with her beau. (*Public domain*)

needle into each pore from which a hair had been plucked. This seems a tad harsh given that there was already a certain amount of discomfort within the sin itself.

Size matters

However, men were also heading for eternal damnation due to their obsession with the size of their shoes. From the late fourteenth century, for around a hundred years, men became enamoured with long pointed shoes called 'Crakows', named for the Polish capital where the style is believed to have originated. The points of these shoes, known as 'poulaines' or 'devil's fingers' by those who disapproved of them, were sometimes so long that they needed to be supported by whalebone or even tied to the wearer's legs with string to stop the shoe tripping up the elegantly dressed poulaine-wearer. Since the length of the shoe was supposed to denote the wealth or class of the wearer – with Edward III decreeing during his 50-year reign between 1327–1377 that common people were only allowed a six-inch toe and gentlemen were allowed fifteenth inches with nobility even longer – many attempted to increase their social cache by lengthening the tips of their poulaines.

Nobility had also long been connected with the height of women's 'hennins', the classic coned headdresses worn in the late Middle Ages. Sometimes this elaborate headgear would be truncated, but some reached the dizzying heights of 36 inches, putting even the most elaborate hats at the modern day races to shame. As if it wasn't enough of a chore to keep such a cumbersome piece of clothing atop your head, the medieval ladies who chose the hennin also had to face fire-and-brimstone preachers. One zealous priest, Friar Thomas Conecte of the Carmelite Order, in 1428 raged against 'the noble ladies, and all others who dressed their heads in so ridiculous a manner, and who expended such large sums on the luxuries of apparel'. He went further and encouraged ill-mannered street urchins to jeer at ladies wearing the hennin and even to pull down their headdresses in the street.

AN   OPTICAL   DELUSION

NEVER MIND BILLY WHAT OTHERS MAY SAY,
YOU ARE VERY PRETTY 'IN MY EYE.

A cruelly satirical cartoon from 1833 depicting the idea that beauty really is in the eye of the beholder. (*Wellcome Library, London*)

A second caricature from 1810 depicting a pairing that illustrates how little looks mattered in the case of a good match. (*Wellcome Library, London*)

Some fashions of the past were exaggerated in order to show that the person wearing these preposterous items was wealthy enough not to work. They didn't have to care about practical clothing considerations. After all, only peasants needed to be able to lift and carry, or indeed walk unimpeded. The wealthy could afford inconvenient frippery and it was a good way of signalling riches, if not always beauty.

Nonetheless, the longest and most incommodious clothing in the world could not guarantee a good match if your countenance lacked intrinsic beauty. Baldassare Castiglione wrote that 'beauty springs from God … and so one cannot have beauty without goodness'. In the past, beauty was perceived quite literally as a virtue.

Such was the obsession with fair looks that even kings and queens were terrified of being tricked into a poor match with an ill-favoured spouse. After all, the only personal qualities the court and political players were interested in were the titles, lands and alliances that a royal marriage could ensure; looks were the last consideration. Besides, we all know the aphorism that beauty is in the eye of the beholder. This was amply proved by the courtship of Elizabeth I and François, Duke of Anjou, which began in the early 1570s and continued for many years.

François was the youngest son of King Henri II of France and Catherine de' Medici. His face was scarred and pitted from a bout of childhood smallpox and his spine was deformed, making him lack stature. Yet, by all contemporary accounts and even her own words, the queen loved the man she referred to as her 'frog'. Although marriage negotiations were never finalised due to the general unpopularity of a French Catholic suitor, Elizabeth confessed that 'I have never in my life seen a creature more agreeable to me'. Alas even kings and queens have to bow to public opinion and Elizabeth was said to have put the needs of the country before that of her own heart.

The poem she is said to have written in 1582 entitled 'On Monsieur's Departure' may well have been about her beloved frog:

I grieve and dare not show my discontent,
I love and yet am forced to seem to hate,
I do, yet dare not say I ever meant,
I seem stark mute but inwardly do prate.
I am and not, I freeze and yet am burned,
Since from myself another self I turned.

My care is like my shadow in the sun,
Follows me flying, flies when I pursue it,
Stands and lies by me, doth what I have done.
His too familiar care doth make me rue it.
No means I find to rid him from my breast,
Till by the end of things it be supprest.

Some gentler passion slide into my mind,
For I am soft and made of melting snow;
Or be more cruel, love, and so be kind.
Let me or float or sink, be high or low.
Or let me live with some more sweet content,
Or die and so forget what love ere meant.

So really the only area in which physical appearance might begin to play a part was if the question arose of whether a royal spouse was healthy enough to sire or bear a child. This was such a pronounced concern that even the powerful Elizabeth I was subjected to a full gynaecological examination in her forties, so that the French could be satisfied that her marriage negotiations with François might still bear fruit. Even when courting royals weren't being subjected to medical examinations, ambassadors were regularly despatched to see the intended when a diplomatic union between states was mooted, to ensure that the prospective king or queen was sufficiently attractive and had no visible deformities or inherited illnesses.

Henry VII sent three representatives to the court of the Queen of Naples in order to ascertain her charms. He gave his envoys an extensive list of characteristics they should note and report back on. These included the royal lady's height, her weight, the size of her breasts, the shape of her nose, the size of her forehead, the shape of her fingers and her age.

However, her physical attributes weren't the only attributes Henry wanted his ambassadors to notice. The more delicate question of how sweet, or sour, her breath smelled and what and how much she ate and drank were also on the list of information to be acquired. After seeking such a plethora of facts about the Queen, it must have been a source of regret to his ambassadors that nothing came of the match – due primarily to political and financial reasons rather than the Queen's failure to match Henry's expectations regarding her beauty.

King Henry VIII, who was famously profligate in the matter of wives, was equally fussy in selecting his spouses. He even sent his chief adviser Thomas Cromwell to the Tower of London over the appearance of one of his brides. Anne of Cleves was not fair enough for the King's tastes and even a pre-nuptial painting by Holbein was not deemed accurate enough when the King finally met his future wife. He went along with the marriage to avoid a rift with the German state from which the young queen originated. However, his discourteous declaration after their wedding night was that she had an unpleasant body odour and her breasts sagged. Six months later he had the marriage annulled and, blaming Cromwell for the whole debacle, had him charged with treason.

Hiding faults

While being beautiful isn't the same thing as being fashionable, many people throughout the ages have aimed to hide a lack of beauty through conspicuously fashion-forward clothing. One of the best fashions for disguising a less than tempting visage was the 'vizard', a mask worn by ladies in the sixteenth and seventeenth centuries in order to protect the skin against the effects of the sun. Vizards could hide a multitude of problems from noses rotted by syphilis to bad skin or pock-marked faces. These masks were often made of dark velvet on the outside to deflect the sun's rays and lined on the inside with silk or perfumed leather. The vizard, when not secured by ribbons to the side, was held in place with a bead on the inside, which women clamped between their teeth.

The somewhat frightening appearance of women wearing vizards was described by Phillip Stubbes, a puritan activist, in his book *Anatomie of Abuses*, published in 1583:

'When thei use to ride abroade, thei have visors made ov Velvet … wherewith thei cover all their faces, havying holes made in them

A 1597 French miniature of a horse-drawn litter carrying a masked lady. (*The British Library*)

against their eyes, Whereout they look So that if a man that knew not their guise before, should chaunce to meete one of them he would think he met a Monster or a Devil: for face he can see none, but two broade holes aginst her eyes, with glasses in them.'

But the fashion was slow to die. As late as summer 1663, the celebrated diarist Samuel Pepys wrote:

'Here [at the Royall Theatre] I saw my Lord Falconbridge, and his Lady, my Lady Mary Cromwell, who looks as well as I have known her, and well clad; but when the House began to fill she put on her vizard, and so kept it on all the play; which of late is become a great fashion among the ladies, which hides their whole face. So to the Exchange, to buy things with my wife; among others, a vizard for herself.'

The vizard was also popular because it had disreputable connotations; it was so routinely worn by courtesans that the term began to be used as a nickname for their profession.

Another beautifying use for black velvet was in the fashion for face patches. Tiny pieces of black velvet or silk were used to create intriguing shapes, such as dots, lozenges, stars and crescents. These were glued to the faces of both men and women. The practice can be traced back to Roman times, but it was most widespread in England in the late seventeenth century, although it had been known during the sixteenth century and remained in use for another hundred years.

Perhaps the reason the trend took such a long time to decline was that it very handily concealed smallpox scars and other disfigurements, if placed wherever an offending blemish was to be found. In Hogarth's *A Harlot's Progress* (1732) series of six plates, plate 3 depicts the prostitute Moll Hackabout wearing face patches while syphilis cures in the room suggest that it is more than fashion that requires her to wear those

A Harlot's Progress (1732), plate 3, an engraving by William Hogarth shows Moll wearing face patches to hide her pox scars. (*Wiki Commons*)

patches. Indeed, the series ends with Moll dying of the disease, which was a common cause of death for women in her profession in the past.

If you were lucky enough to be using patches purely to draw attention to your best features, there were names for each of the most advantageous positions. Sarah Jane Downing writes in *Beauty and Cosmetics 1550-1950* (2012), 'The "coquette" was situated near to a pretty smile, the "passionate" at the corner of the eye, and the "gallant" as a dimple in the middle of the cheek.'

It was not just women who engaged in patching, as the fashionable man about town was considered equally dashing when adorned with a patch. 'If it be a lover's part you are to act, take a black spot or two; twill make your face more amorous, and appear more gracious in your mistress's eyes,' wrote playwright, Henry Glapthorne in 1640.

As well as the continuing use of patches, there was much danger in attempting to look beautiful through artificial means. Lead within ceruse and powders regularly caused swollen eyes, receding gums and even premature death. In 1760 Lady Coventry, née Maria Gunning, a great reputed beauty, died of lead poisoning from her make-up. Her sister, Lady Elizabeth Hamilton, was also taken severely ill from using ceruse but

A coloured lithograph from 1865 showing three women with plaited and ringletted hair along with five plaited and ringletted hairpieces. (*Wellcome Library, London*)

survived – although not with her looks intact. The death of the celebrated courtesan Kitty Fisher was also linked to beautifying with lead.

In less severe cases, the lead-based make-up merely caused facial hair to thin or fall out completely, thereby necessitating the use of fake eyebrows made from the hide of mice. In the seventeenth century, plumpers were another beauty aid. These were small balls or discs made of cork, used to plump out the cheeks so that hollows made by missing teeth could be disguised. Then there were artificial teeth made from hippo ivory and even human teeth from either live impoverished donors or dead soldiers from battlefields such as Waterloo in 1815. Even the first president of the United States, George Washington (1732-1799) had a set of human teeth screwed into hippo ivory dentures. Finally, of course, there were also extravagant wigs to hide receding hairlines and thinning hair.

Although men, just as much as women, took advantage of these crafty methods of enhancement, as is often the case, they were not the butt of jokes in quite the same way. The poet Matthew Price wrote this cruel little verse about mice hide eyebrows in 1718:

> 'Helen was just slipt into bed
> Her eyebrows on the toilet lay
> Away the kitten with them fled
> As fees belonging to her prey.'

It is believed that 'false parts' ballads have been composed since antiquity, with several long versions becoming popular in the seventeenth and eighteenth centuries. The narratives of these ballads usually involved a suitor being tricked into pursuing a comely maiden, who turned out to be an ugly hag once she had removed her false parts, such as a glass eye, a peg leg, or a wig masking her baldness. The more honest ballads had the young man appeased with the 'old hag's treasure chest', reinforcing the message that money was often the virtue selected over natural youth or beauty.

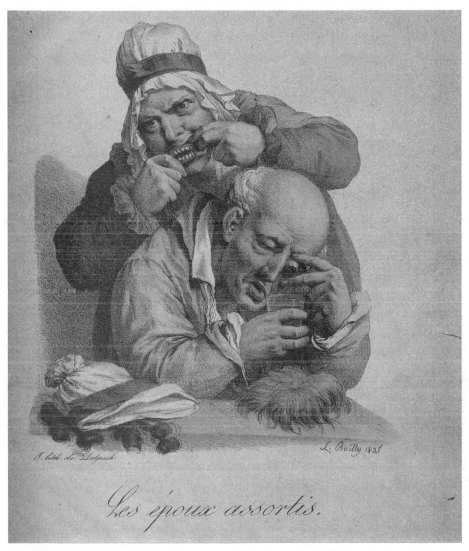

Les époux assortis.

An 1825 lithograph depicting a couple assembling their false body parts: false teeth, a glass eye and wigs. (*Wellcome Library, London*)

The terror of being tricked by a lover's falsely constructed exterior was probably exacerbated by the Church. Early Christian writer, Tertullian, who charmingly described women as 'the doorway to the devil', wrote that they should 'have their eyes painted with chastity, the word of

God inserted in their ears, Christ's yoke tied to their hair, and subject themselves to their husbands'. Make-up was often described not just as 'peynting' but also 'counterfeiting', emphasising that beauty that was artificial was some form of trickery.

Count Castiglione, despite hailing from the more liberal sixteenth century Italian court, wrote in *The Book of the Courtier* (c.1516–18):

> 'Surely you realise how much more graceful a woman is who, if indeed she wishes to do so, paints herself so sparingly and so little that whoever looks at her is unsure whether she is made-up or not, in comparison with one whose face is so encrusted that she seems to be wearing a mask and who dare not laugh for fear of causing it to crack ... letting herself be seen only by torchlight, in the way a wily merchant shows his cloth in a dark corner ... such is the uncontrived simplicity which is most attractive to the eyes and minds of men, who are always afraid of being tricked by art.'

Philip Stubbes, who wrote so disapprovingly of vizards, was also horrified by make-up, writing:

> 'Saint Ciprian, amongst the rest, saith, a woman, through painting and dying her face, sheweth herselfe to be more then whorish. For (saith he) she hath corrupted and defaced (like a filthie strumpet or brothel) the workmanship of god in her, what is this els but to turn truth into falsehoode, with painting and slibbersauces?'

Stubbes should have taken more care over his choice of words, for the Elizabethans had by then followed the example of their queen, with women painting their faces with ceruse and alabaster and rouging their cheeks, in imitation of their 'faerie queen'.

Elizabeth I, painted in c.1600 by an unknown artist, was a great role model for fashions of the age. (*National Portrait Gallery, London*)

Fashion and frippery

Just as a woman's use of make-up could indicate how attentively she had listened to the edicts of the Church, so too could her wardrobe. Queen Mary I, who set about the restoration of the Catholic Church in 1553, dressed dourly for her reign, leading the Venetian ambassador to say of her: 'She is a saint. She dresses badly.' By contrast Elizabeth I wore sumptuous capes and heavily embellished gowns in order to show that her reign was to be significantly different from that of her half-sister.

The writings of Margaret Fell, one of the founding members of the Religious Society of Friends (also known as Quakers) who was born eleven years after the death of Elizabeth I, show that by the late seventeenth century religious interference in the appearance of women was still a concern. She spoke out against the Christian sect's later obsession with plain clothing restrictions. 'This is a silly, poor Gospel. It is more fit for us to be covered with God's eternal spirit, and clothed with his Eternal light.'

It was not just the pious who wanted a say in how people were dressing. Trade meant that news was always coming into Britain from the continent of how the fashionable French and Italian courts were carrying on and, later, colonialism would yield far better clothing options in the form of Indian shawls and silks.

The well-heeled crowd had increasing opportunities to show their exalted position in the social strata through the medium of clothes and fine accessories, such as fans and gloves. For example, the seventeenth century heralded the development of the folded fan, whereas previously fans had been fixed. While aristocrats could afford these new fripperies, less well-off ladies had to content themselves with the feathered fixed fans of earlier times. By the eighteenth century, imports from the Far East and the development of cheaper printed fans had made folded fans affordable for a wider number of ladies.

As the middle classes struggled to keep up with their economic superiors in the matter of style, the changes that the Industrial Revolution in the

FULL DRESS

PARISIAN LADIES in their **WINTER DRESS** for **1800**

This 1799 satirical caricature print entitled *Parisian Ladies in their Full Winter Dress for 1800* by Isaac Cruikshank (1756–1811) shows how scandalously revealing the British found the Parisian high Greek look.

mid–eighteenth century brought in must have been something of a relief. For this emerging class, it was deemed far more moral to be prudent and self-made than profligate and privileged. Nevertheless, many in the middle classes were still very much interested in social climbing through acquired wealth, connections or appearances.

In Austen's *Pride and Prejudice* (1813), the well-dressed Bingley sisters are very haughty toward the Bennets when they learn that their maternal

"ARABELLA MARIA. "Only to think, Julia dear, that our Mothers wore such ridiculous fashions as these!"
BOTH. "Ha! ha! ha! ha!"

Two women, wearing full crinolines, mock the neo-Grecian attire of their Regency mothers. Satirical cartoon from the 11 July 1857 issue of *Harper's Weekly* (New York).

uncle Mr Gardiner is in trade rather than a gentleman like Mr. Bennet. Austen wittily gives the proud pair a nouveau-riche background that shows their snobbery for the hypocrisy it really is:

'They were of a respectable family in the north of England; a circumstance more deeply impressed on their memories than that their brother's fortune and their own had been acquired by trade.'

Fashions also had a knack of recurring in the past, just as they do today. 'Imbecile sleeves' gained their dreadful name because they were often so large that it would be difficult for a woman wearing them to get through a narrow doorway. The real name for these puffy sleeves was 'gigot', from the French, meaning the hind leg of an animal, such as a sheep or a lamb – literally 'mutton leg' sleeve. They were hugely puffy at the top until the elbow, where they tapered in and tightly hugged the arm from the elbow to the wrist.

First seen in the sixteenth century, these impractical sleeves returned to favour in the early nineteenth century. In the 1830s they were used to create the sloped shoulder silhouette much in favour and, by the 1890s, the Victorian obsession with hourglass figures was also served well by this fashion.

Throughout the ages the ideal formula for 'beauty' has regularly changed her dimensions and qualities. From the high foreheads and pious oval egg-shaped faces of the early Middle Ages to the Victorian low hairlines and tight ringlets framing pale faces and dark eyes, fashion ran the gamut of female variety. You had to be lucky indeed to be born with the correct attributes to be deemed a beauty in your time.

Books giving advice on such matters abounded from the earliest times, with ancient Roman poet Ovid writing in *The Art of Love* that a woman should take care to remove body hair:

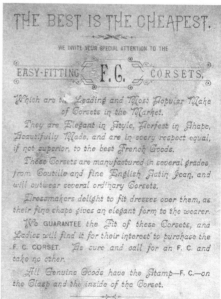

American clothing trading cards used to advertise the latest must-have fashions of the Victorian era. (*Boston Public Library*)

Fitz Herbert having bought this Stylish Suit at the "CONTINENTAL," is now so irresistible that the girls all want to go home with him. [COPYRIGHTED.]   OVER.

This Victorian American clothing advertisement claims that a gentleman will become irresistible to women if he purchases a suit from the Continental clothing store. (*Boston Public Library*)

> 'A stubbled leg your suitor will not charm,
> And–dare I warn?– no goat below the arm.'

Given how much work had to be put into becoming a 'natural' beauty, one would have hoped the writers and critics of times gone by would have been less severe upon those who used artifice and subterfuge to make the most of what they had. For love is not always quite as blind as one would hope.

Chapter Three

Love Tokens and Gifts

Acceptable gifts from lovers and admirers

There is an old English saying from the mid-nineteenth century that 'kissing's out of fashion when gorse is out of bloom'. Given that gorse can be in flower throughout the year, this implies that you can always find love and romance.

The real challenge in days gone by was not in the kissing itself, but in finding an opportunity for it. If you were poor, you had work to attend to and so couldn't idle away the time in love-making. Most of those in service might only enjoy one afternoon off work per month and a lack of leisure time is a hindrance in courting. If you were rich, then there was pressure to refine all the accomplishments that a young lady was considered to need in order to make herself a good match.

The competition among debutantes and older single ladies was fierce, as shown by entries in Alice Miles's diary, published posthumously in *Every Girl's Duty: Diary of a Victorian Debutante* (1993):

> "… there is Mrs Verschoyle; a very pretty brunette of two and thirty … Miss Castor who I met in London, forty and painfully plain, familiarly known as the Camel. Miss Ogle, commonly called 'The Ghoul'…who cannot be more repulsive looking – she says she's twenty-three, if so I am very sorry for her … there's a rather pretty little heiress Miss Harriet Ives Wright … who I suspect will put us all in the shade from the mere fact of her possessing £4,000 a year."

The same source gives us an insight into a typical day for a Victorian debutante. Alice Miles usually rose late from bed to recover from the night before, then lunched at home or out with friends and then took an afternoon chaperoned stroll or ride out in the carriage at Hyde Park. This routine might be followed by 'morning' calls, which were really formalised visits at which one could leave calling cards. A relaxed five o'clock tea then gave way to hours of getting ready for a formal dinner at around eight or nine o'clock. This would end in the ladies retiring to the drawing room and the gentlemen smoking cigars and enjoying a cognac. It would only be later that the sexes would come together to play at cards and practise their flirtations. Other post-dinner enjoyments included concerts or even a ball, which would start at midnight and finish at four or five in the morning. All this definitely resulted in a need for a lie-in for the wealthy and pretty lady-about-town!

The social season for a debutante ran during Parliamentary recess from Easter until August and comprised races, river parties, regattas and picnics. In the autumn there would be shooting and country house parties to attend. While there was plenty of opportunity to see your preferred suitor in company, a private audience could not be hoped for. So, what to do in the interim, when thoughts arose about your suitor? In such cases, a love token or gift was the ideal solution. A man could look upon the hair in a ring and a woman could caress the gloves her intended had sent her.

Giving presents to one's paramour was a tricky business. If you weren't yet betrothed or you had good reason to hide your courtship, then it was necessary to choose gifts with care. Although an example of a fabulously guileless and sweet courting gift was the small orphaned lamb that Gabriel Oak takes as a gift to Bathsheba in the hope his offer of marriage might be accepted in Thomas Hardy's *Far From The Madding Crowd* (1874). Farmer Oak takes no pains to hide his feelings for Bathsheba alerting her aunt to the proposed match and ensuring she discourages him in the first instance before Bathsheba deals a second, more fatal, blow to his hopes. While in this case the charmingly artless farmer felt no need to hide his intentions, a serviceman about to go off to war, for example, would often delay an engagement until his return to ensure that, should he not return, waiting to hear of his fate would not unduly restrict his fiancée.

Hair was the perfect answer to a lover's quandary. A lock of hair was a sign of fidelity when given as a lovers' keepsake, but conversely it could provide a sentimental reminder of deceased loved ones. By the Victorian era, you could conceivably wear a piece of jewellery with hair inside it or inlaid within the design, because you were mourning a close relative or perhaps as a memento of a much-loved sister while you were away from home. Hair could be easily disguised, as remembrance was the perfect camouflage if you had a lover whose existence you would rather not reveal. Although one disturbing example was that of Lady Caroline Lamb sending Lord Byron a bloodied clump of her pubic hair! However, it must be said that discretion wasn't really that lady's forte, having made her affair with the poet quite public despite being married to the Whig politician Lord Melbourne.

The more discreet wealthy beau could hide his intent in coded rings called acrostic rings. The first letter of each gem inlaid within the ring would spell out a word such as 'regard', 'love' or 'dear' or a significant date. Only those in the know would realise that the ring had a special message in its setting.

For women, it must have been doubly difficult to hide a secret love for a shiny new piece of jewellery would have set tongues a-wagging. Presents of perishables such as fruit or flowers would perhaps have been more welcome, even if you'd only be able to press a flower or two to keep as a reminder of your lover's regard for you.

The Victorians were fond of the language of flowers or 'floriography', in which the selection of blooms in a bouquet could symbolise particular qualities and demonstrate your regard – or lack thereof – for the lady in question. For example flowers to avoid were: Columbine (folly), Lavender (mistrust), Morning Glory (affection), Narcissus (egotism), Oleander (beware) and Yellow Carnations (rejection). As we saw earlier with the language of fans and precious stones, this seems to have been restricted to the wealthy and largely a female affectation. In any case, rural suitors would have been severely restricted in the choice of wild flowers they might pick for a bouquet.

More serious men mocked the whole idea of flower symbolism, with H G Wells writing in 1897, 'In these days we season our love-making

These illustrations from *The Language of Flowers: An Alphabet of Floral Emblems* (1857) show what each flower in a bouquet meant to Victorians.

with talk about heredity, philanthropy, and sanitation, and present one another with Fabian publications instead of wild flowers. But in the end, I fancy the business comes to very much the same thing.'

A wonderful tradition, found among the Pennsylvanian Quakers in the United States in the eighteenth and early nineteenth centuries, was that

The love token created by Hugh Pugh for Mary Fisher in 1801. (*Photo courtesy: Meg Schultz*)

of true lover's knots. These were paper tokens written in such a way that they would form intelligible sentences all the way around the squares of paper, no matter which way they were read. One of the best examples of this is that of teacher Hugh Pugh's lover's knot made for Mary Fisher, one of his pupils in Bedford County, Pennsylvania.

In a precursor to the textspeak we now find widespread, Pugh also shortened phrases, for example 'CU' meaning 'see you'. Alas Mary, while she must have liked the poetry enough to keep the token and hand it down to her granddaughter, married a farmer and, by all accounts, broke poor Hugh's heart. The knot was also a marriage proposal, but in the typical petulance of spurned lovers past and present, he says that she will be an 'inconstant creature' with a 'double heart' if she turns him down.

Meg Schultz, great-great-great granddaughter of Mary Fisher, now owns the artefact and kindly gave me permission to reproduce it here. While Mary Fisher was not won over by Hugh's indubitable artistry, the token is even more spectacular when you consider that Meg's research turned up that he only had one hand.

Here is the transcript of the Pugh–Fisher lover's knot:

'A true Lovers Knot to thee my Dear I send, An Emblem of true Love without an end, Crossing turning, winding in and out, Never ceasing turning round about. And as thee sees its Linkes and Crosses here, so hath thy Beauty prov'd to me a Snare, By observation of true Love I find I am bereaved of both ♥ and mind.

Most lovely fair one look with pity down, And do not on thy faithful Lover frown, But pardon him who ever doth thy Love desire, And ever will thy Beauteous form admire.

Therefore thou Lovely fair one let thy Beauty shine, With Beams of Comfort ravishing and divine, That so my raving Soul may by thy Love, Pass into Bliss if we both constant prove, Then shall these Crosses in this Knot of Love, Be all disdain'd if thou consenting prove.

Here is an Impression of my ♥ thee may see, Within this Knot that I present, to thee, Therefore thee may imagine that I am in grief, And none but thee can yield to me Relief, My ravished Soul doth ever long to see, The Marriage Knot so firmly ty'd between thee and me.

(*Top centre circle*)

Why do I Love, go ask
the Alerious Sun
Why every Day he around the World doth run
Ask Thames and Tiber why they Ebb and flow
Ask Damask Roses why in June they grow.
They shew to us how everything doth move
Thus teaching them to that, and me
to Love.
Mary Fisher
Bedford County Decem'r 9th
1801

(*Right circle*)

There is but one
And only one
And I am only he
That loves but one
And only one
And thou art the only she
Requite me with like love again
And say thus unto me —
There is but one, And only one
And thou art the only he.
Mary Fisher

(*Bottom centre circle*)

Accept lovely fair Maid
From thy neighbor and friend
Each wish that can friendship endear
May the bounty of Heaven propitiously endear
Long Life and Happy each Year.
May every enjoyment which prudence allow
Thy Life Long continue to Bless —
May Love and Esteem
Weave a Wreath for thy Brow
And thy Beauty be crown'd with Success.
Mary Fisher

(*Left circle*)

As soon grief shall
sink into my ♥
2CUX my Love without desert (?)
You have a ♥, a double ♥, I fear.
2 great a X of ♥ oh ♥ forbear
AX, AX, ICUB,
A double XU are to me.

H Pugh [Monogram]

This Ring is round
And hath no end
So is my Love
To thee my Friend
Mary Fisher

(Diagonal rectangle, top left)

Here I dare venture with my Love a lot (?)
In Half an Hour she does not read my Knot

(Diagonal rectangle, top right)

And if she wins I'll freely pay my Debt,
But if she loses then I'll claim my Bett.

(Diagonal rectangle bottom right)

As for description, A begins thee will find,
E Ends the same, be constant in thy mind.

(Diagonal rectangle, bottom left)

Lovers well know what it is to part,
When between 2 Lovers there is but one ♥

H Pugh [Monogram]

(8 small outer boxes)

My ♥ you have
Your ♥ I crave

My ♥ you have
Confin'd

And leaves all other
Hearts behind.

(4 tiny corner diagonal boxes)

If thou refuse me

I must say
thou art

An unconstant
Creature

With a double ♥

Handmade or mass-produced?

The nineteenth century was also the age of the mass-produced Valentine's card, allowing men for the first time to purchase rather than make a hand-crafted card for the ladies they admired. Not only were there beautiful confections of cards with cut-outs and textiles, there were even horribly cruel versions to punish a lover who had rejected you. These often made use of the 'false parts' idea to accuse the recipient of being a fake beauty or of some character default. Called a 'Vinegar Valentine', understandably few examples of these survive.

One rare vinegar Valentine's card, showing a cartoon of a woman with a large nose, was inscribed:

> *'On account of your talk of others' affairs*
> *At most dances you sit warming the chairs.*
> *Because of the care with which you attend*
> *To all others' business you haven't a friend.'*

Doubtless a lady who received one of those would think she had had a lucky escape, if she discovered which rogue had sent her it.

Rustic traditions put a great deal more art into courtship gifts. Intricate carvings were painstakingly created for sweethearts in Wales, where elaborate hand-made love spoons became popular during the seventeenth century, as well as in other parts of Europe. The spoons had the dual purpose of showing a girl's father a suitor's woodworking skills, as well as charming the lady as evidence of the time spent meticulously carving something just for her. There was also an intimacy inherent within the utensil, as a spoon would touch your beloved's mouth. Yet, over time the spoons became so elaborate that they ceased to have a practical function and began to be used as wall hangings.

Each symbol carved into a love spoon had a special meaning. Anchors were often prevalent as sailors would carve their spoons while on long sea voyages. Bells indicated marriage, hearts, of course, denoted love and a horseshoe stood for luck. The practice of being able

A modern carved wooden love spoon token from the author's own collection.

to carve caged balls into the spoon's handle was said to indicate how many children were hoped for in the union.

In some parts of northern England and Scotland, knitting sheaths or sticks were regarded as love tokens. These beautifully engraved objects were very useful for those who gained a second income from knitting or had to clothe their families, as the sheath would ensure you could knit one-handed while doing other things, such as walking to market or even while engaging in farm work. At this time men also frequently knitted to help supplement the family income.

Some men would carve the names of their sweethearts into the sticks they themselves used and tuck them into their belts as they knitted. Their ladies must have experienced a frisson of excitement to see their name so close to their beloved's body.

It was this idea of second-hand physical contact that also made stay busks or corset stiffeners popular engraved gifts for women. Worn right by the heart, under the breast, it was a romantic gift that held the promise of future intimacy for both suitor and the lady being wooed.

In the courtly tradition, there were, however, some gifts considered disreputable. André Le Chapelain, presumed to be a courtier in Marie de Champagne's court, wrote in his twelfth century book, *About Love*, that the more conventional gifts for a woman in love, which she might receive without her reputation being tarnished, included: 'a handkerchief, a wreath of gold or silver, a mirror, a purse, a comb, a picture and a washbasin'. A washbasin seems a somewhat conspicuous gift, especially as Le Chapelain also advises that a ring given by a lover should be worn on the smallest finger of the left hand, since that hand is more likely to be out of sight. If one must take care to hide a lover's ring, surely a great big washbasin would be a giveaway?

As the fashion for courtly love began to be pastiched by artists and writers, in the mid-thirteenth century, Ulrich von Lichtenstein wrote *Frauendient* [In the Service of Ladies] in which the protagonist – a knight-errant – cuts off his finger and sends it as a gift to the lady he serves. Not unsurprisingly she fails to be wooed by his attentions, and so he sets off wandering from Venice to Vienna while dressed as Venus in white gowns with braided hair and duelling all-comers for the honour of his lady.

In the United States, historic love tokens were not quite so eccentric. A popular form was quite literally a token: a coin with the sides polished off and hand-engraved with names, dates and messages. Easy to carry around or make into pieces of jewellery such as bracelets and pins, the tokens made for popular presents. They also had symbolic pictures engraved on them, such as a bluebird for happiness or a forget-me-not for enduring affection.

Gifts were important not just for wooing, but in order to prove a couple's intentions towards one another. As we saw earlier, marriages in earlier periods did not need a member of the clergy or parental consent, if the couple were of age and made their declarations before witnesses. This didn't change in England and Wales until Lord Hardwicke's Marriage Act came into effect in 1754 and decreed a formal marriage ceremony take place in order for a marriage to be valid. The official name of this legislation is *An Act for the Better Preventing of Clandestine Marriage*.

A famous Tudor case of a marriage contracted in the earlier manner is of William Hanwell and Isabel Riddysdale. On 1 January 1519, the couple pledged their troth to each other at a house in Beachampton, Buckinghamshire, making them husband and wife. When Isabel subsequently regretted her decision and refused to honour her vows, William took her to the church court and produced two witnesses to the union. One witness revealed that he had entrusted him with two pennies that were to be given to Isabel as a love token. This was seen as proof of the couple's intention to marry.

An engraved German or Austrian coin from the late nineteenth century, popularly given as love tokens, with mounting brackets for wearing in a brooch or necklace. (*Flickr Creative Commons Licence: Jerry "Woody", Canada*)

A problem with receiving gifts is that this creates an obligation to a gentleman or lady that you are not interested in. Samuel Beeton, husband to the famous Mrs. Isabella Beeton, writes at length about this subject in his *Complete Etiquette for Ladies* (1876):

'In her intercourse with gentlemen a lady should take care to avoid all pecuniary obligation. The civility which a gentleman conventionally owes to a lady is a sufficient tax – more she has no right to expect or accept. A man of good sense and of true politeness will not be offended at her unwillingness to become his debtor. On the contrary, he will respect her delicacy and approve her dignity, and consent at once to her becoming her own banker on all occasions where expense is to be incurred.'

So it seems that the notion of a man paying for dinner on the first date is not in any way linked to historical ideas of chivalry.

Beeton goes on to counsel a woman to only accept invitations to amusements if she is permitted to pay for her own ticket, handing over her share of the bill to the gentleman before he leaves. This fastidious attention to staying financially independent extends to gifts as well.

'We disapprove of ladies going to charity fairs in the evening, when they require a male escort, and when that escort is likely to be drawn into paying exorbitant prices for gifts to his fair companion – particularly if induced to do so from the fear of appearing mean or of being thought wanting in benevolence.'

He is equally stern in the matter of women's behaviour in shops while accompanied by a suitor:

'When visiting a fancy shop with a gentleman, refrain from excessively admiring any handsome or expensive article you may chance to see there; above all, express no wish that you were able to buy it, and to regret that you cannot, lest he should construe these extreme tokens of admiration into hints that you wish him to buy it for you. To allow him to do so would, on your part, be very mean and indelicate, and on his very foolish.'

Samuel Beeton may have written harshly against those women who angled for gifts from gentlemen, but present-giving is an essential part of wooing and what girl wouldn't want to wear a ribbon bought by her beau? After all, not every woman will receive presents as extravagant as the ones Louis XV bestowed on his mistress, the Countess du Barry, who was given a château as a throwaway gift to entice her to spend the evening with him.

Writing in the more censorious nineteenth century, however, Beeton advises his lady-readers that 'no gentleman who really respects her will offer her anything more than a bouquet, a book, one or two autographs of distinguished persons, or a few relics or mementoes of memorable places – things that derive their chief value from associations.' Jewellery, articles of clothing and costly ornaments 'ought to be regarded as an offence rather than a compliment, excusable only in a man sadly ignorant of the refinements of society'.

In fact several anonymous Victorian etiquette writers suggested that no gift should ever been given to a lady unless an offer of marriage has been made and she has accepted it.

But what was a woman to do if she was offered a present by a suitor who had not yet made her an offer? Samuel Beeton is unequivocal: 'she should set him right, and civilly, but firmly refuse to be his debtor.' Equally, if, for whatever reason, a courtship or betrothal ended, 'a gentleman should return all presents, letters and other tokens of regard'.

Chapter Four

Coxcombs and Strumpets

*How to recognise roguish men and women of ill repute –
and how to avoid them*

Courting is often seen as gentle, chaste romance – a precursor to staid and secure marriage. The truth is that almost a third of all Elizabethan brides entered the church already pregnant. There was plenty of illicit sex being enjoyed, but alas only the rural poor accepted it as a custom to check the fertility of a bride-to-be. It was an extremely risky activity for a woman to engage in if she belonged to the upper or middle classes.

The hand-wringing and upheaval of Lydia Bennet's elopement is vividly depicted in Jane Austen's *Pride and Prejudice* (1813). Perhaps the most chilling words of the entire book are within Uncle Gardiner's letter to Mr Bennet: 'I have seen them both. They are not married, nor can I find there was any intention of being so; but if you are willing to perform the engagements which I have ventured to make on your side, I hope it will not be long before they are.'

It is clear from Lydia's earlier letter to Mrs Forster that she had believed she was eloping to be married at Gretna Green, but is later convinced by Wickham to go to London, as yet unmarried. Elizabeth Bennet takes some little comfort in the discovery that Lydia was not party to 'a scheme of infamy'. While her sister may have been wild and rebellious, even she knew that the only respectable way to be with a man in society was to ultimately marry him.

The newly emerging middle classes in Regency England were loath to emulate the dissolute lifestyle of the Prince Regent and his cronies.

'The Elopement' by Edmund Blair Leighton, 1893. (*Public domain*)

These 1911 postcards imagine what a Gretna Green elopement must have been like during the Regency period. (*Public domain*)

Reputation played a vital role in establishing that a daughter of the gentry was marriageable. What would have become of Lydia after her elopement had Wickham not been bribed to marry her?

What is certain is that she would not have been allowed to re-enter polite society and the marriage prospects of her sisters would also have been severely damaged. The colourful case of Lady Sarah Lennox illustrates this quite succinctly. The debutante poised to perhaps become a future queen of England ended up the victim of her own romantic inclinations. While George III looked fondly on her, her family's ambitions ensured that he was pushed away from considering her a suitable mate. It was only after she married Charles Bunbury in 1762 that her own actions rather than those of her family started to impact on her social status. While a discreet affair could be hushed up, Lady Lennox not only had an affair with Lord William Gordon, but also had an illegitimate child with him – a daughter named Louisa, born in 1768. Given that neither her or her child were disowned by her husband, she could perhaps have got away with the adultery, were it not for the fact that she subsequently ran away with Gordon, taking Louisa with her. Alas her lover soon rejected her and she was forced to live with her brother since her husband would not take her back and applied for a divorce on the grounds of adultery, ignoring the fact of Louisa's parentage. A divorce was granted on 14 May 1776, despite Lady Sarah's protestations. With her reputation in tatters, most eligible matches would now be beyond her, but she ended up remarrying an impoverished – and therefore not entirely desirable – army officer.

Men – and their female relations – kept a hawk-like eye out for any report of impropriety in a potential mate. It didn't have to be as dramatic as an elopement such as that of Lady Sarah Lennox, even the suggestion of being an indelicate sort would be enough to render a woman unappealing – after all, no man wanted to run the risk of being cuckolded or paying for a child whose parentage was questionable. Although it is as well to point out that wealth was a virtue that could balance out a multitude of sins.

The extremely wealthy heiress Seymour Dorothy Fleming married Sir Richard Worsley at the tender age of seventeen in 1775, but then six years later eloped with his friend Captain George Bisset. The resulting scandal did not bring into the public eye the question of Lady Worsley's child by George Bisset, but there is little else it didn't cover. Salacious details of the marriage and Seymour's infidelities were revealed in the press when Worsley brought an action against Bisset for criminal conversation, a law under which a husband could claim damages from a third party who he believed had debauched his wife. While he was suing for £20,000, a vast sum, the jury awarded him just a shilling when evidence surfaced that Worsley had encouraged and connived in his wife's affairs for the purposes of titillation. The judge even concluded that Lady Worsley had been 'prostituted' for at least four years by her husband who participated willingly in his cuckolding.

The press loved one detail in which a maid at the baths overheard Worsley encouraging Bisset to climb on his shoulders in order to look through a window at his naked wife changing at the baths. Mary Marriott, the bathing attendant in question, reported that she heard Worsley call out: "Seymour! Seymour! Bisset is going to get up and look at you!"

Sadly, despite Seymour enduring public humiliation in the cause of George Bisset, he left her for a younger woman shortly after the trial – despite her being pregnant again with him. The fate of the

James Gillray's hand-coloured etching, published 14 March 1782, entitled 'Sir Richard Worse-than-sly, exposing his wife's bottom – O Fye!' (*National Portrait Gallery*)

child is unknown, suspected stillborn, and the earlier child that Richard Worsley had adopted, had died during the trial. Even her legitimate son by Worsley died before his parents at the age of nineteen. Shunned by her family and by those who fancied themselves 'respectable', Seymour left for France once her separation was settled, a settlement that obliged her not to return to England for four years – a dangerously unfortunate clause given that it meant she had to lay low in France at the time of the French Revolution when aristocrats were being routinely guillotined. She survived and even married a man 20 years her junior after Worsley died. In a fitting reversal of tradition, her husband took her name of Fleming after their marriage.

Character and virtue

Such aristocratic examples of debauched wives and shocking husbands made the middle classes very uneasy; making a good match was no longer just ensuring that the prospective husband or wife had wealth but also that they were of good character. By the late 1830s, the Victorians had a comprehensive code of behaviour that ensured ladies were not just respectable, but *seen* to be so. As we'll see in the next chapter, chaperons were a very important part of this.

So how were virtuous young women to tell a Wickham from a Darcy? Roguish men who were only after one thing were not unheard of and being able to seduce a young heiress was a surefire way to bag a fortune. It was for this reason that heiresses were so assiduously protected by their guardians, while relatively poor women, such as Lydia Bennet and her like, had more freedom.

Young women eager to protect their virtue had plenty of authors willing to proffer advice, if lacking a mother's guidance.

In *The Young Lady's Friend*, published in 1838 by an anonymous married American author, the young lady in question is counseled to 'not be afraid to refuse the acquaintance of a known libertine, it is a tribute which you owe to virtue, and, if generally paid, would do more to purify society, and keep the moral standard of it high, than the laws of the land or the eloquence of the pulpit'.

Men were also subject to self-help manuals, such as *The Gentlemen's Book of Etiquette*, published in 1875, which contains some very sound advice on how to speak about the object of one's affections:

> 'It is only the most arrant coxcomb who will boast of the favor shown him by a lady, speak of her by her first name, or allow others to jest with him upon his friendship or admiration for her. If he really admires her, and has reason to hope for a future engagement with her, her name should be as sacred to him as if she were already his wife; if, on the contrary, he is not on intimate terms with her, then he adds a lie to his excessively bad breeding, when using her name familiarly.'

American commentators were painfully aware of how a more open attitude to courting could give rise to a variety of ills. *The Bazar Book of Decorum*, published in 1870, carried 'A Warning about Fast Girls':

> 'The free eye is a marked characteristic of the libertine, and all modest women should turn persistently from its roving and unlicensed glances. Some girls of the *fast* kind, with an audacious defiance of conventional propriety, and yet often with no thought of offense against real modesty, will not only recklessly dally with these intrusive looks, but not seldom venture a cast of them on their own account.
>
> 'There are fast women everywhere, but the fast girl seems to be more particularly an American product. A tendency on the part of the young, unmarried female to eccentric flights of any kind is effectually checked in most countries by parental control.

'It is, moreover, a paltry ambition, and not without risk to virtue, to aspire to the distinction of being pointed out as 'the low-necked' Bel Smith, or the 'high-stepping' Fanny Jones, or the girl who drank a whole bottle of champagne, or she who smoked one of Frank Tripup's fifty-cent regalia...Her essential defect is a vulgar ambition for notoriety. She will endure any thing but obscurity, and therefore takes care that she is seen, heard, and talked of by all the world. Her dress is accordingly flaunting, her voice loud, her words slangy, her eye staring, her manners obtrusive, and conduct audaciously irregular. All this may be, and is, doubtless, done without any overt act of vice, but it looks so much like it that the difference is hardly perceptible to the external observer. In fact, it seems to be the purpose of the fast damsel to assume the semblance of wickedness...

'It would seem that American parents might curtail somewhat the liberty of their children, without interfering too much with that independence of action so essential to the strength of character. Girls are allowed to consider themselves women too soon, and are thus prematurely emancipated from parental control...with less idle time and more watchful parental care, there would be fewer of those fast girls...'

The worry was that a 'fast girl' would make for a capricious and flirtatious wife, thereby making her husband look ridiculous. However, the attractiveness of such girls meant that many men ended up trapped in marriages to women who had been fun to court, but were not suitable spouses. Avoiding such a situation was behind much of the advice given to young men of the era, whether published or oft-repeated in the parlours.

If Americans were preoccupied by 'fast girls', the British Victorians were far more concerned with keeping distinctions of class and money in place. An heiress could be as fast as she liked and still attract suitors, but poorer girls could not hope for such indulgence.

The idea that less well-off women could not be 'delicate' or that they were more primitive or base has historically been given much credence

A stolen kiss depicted in Francesco Hayez's 'The Kiss', 1859. (*The Yorck Project*)

by male authors. André le Chapelain writing in the twelfth century, believed that the rules of love did not apply to farmers who he claimed resembled the beasts they cared for, by freely giving themselves up to lust as nature intended. He counsels against allowing farmers to form

LA PROSTITUTION CONTEMPORAINE

III. — LE LUPANAR ARISTOCRATIQUE.

Elles se rangent sur deux files. Le miché sérieux fait son entrée. Toutes lui
envoient des regards brûlants, se dandinent, prennent des positions excitantes,
sourient... — *(Page 109).*

A well–dressed client inspects the prostitutes at a brothel, 1884. (*Wellcome Library, London*) the finer feelings, in case this should make them too weak to fulfil their purpose of producing food for the community.

He also openly advises labourers to rape any lower class woman who takes their fancy, since her 'shyness' needs to be overcome. 'And if you should, by chance, fall in love with some of their women, be careful to puff them up with lots of praise and then, when you find a convenient place, do not hesitate to take what you seek and to embrace them by force.' Given that this advice is coming from a clergyman, one can see the open contempt that the nobility had for the peasantry. They were perceived as little more than animals to abuse and abandon.

In 1728, John Gay wrote *The Beggar's Opera*, a satirical ballad opera, which in one verse presented the sanitised view of prostitutes: as young girls abandoned and forced to sell sex on the streets of Covent Garden:

> *Virgins are like the fair flower in its lustre,*
> *Which in the garden enamels the ground;*
> *Near it the bees in play flutter and cluster,*
> *And gaudy butterflies frolic around;*
> *But, when once pluck'd, 'tis no longer alluring,*
> *To Covent-garden 'tis sent, (as yet sweet).*
> *There fades and shrinks, and grows past all enduring,*
> *Rots, stinks, and dies, and is trod under feet.*

Harris's List of Covent Garden Ladies, published between 1757 and 1795, seems to almost gleefully and titillatingly document the fall of women who were seduced and abandoned by men. For example a Miss Les-r of 23 Upper Newman Street has this entry:

'This lady was a few years since, a servant in a gentleman's family, near Holborn: in which capacity she used frequently to walk for the air, with her little ward, in Gray's Inn Gardens. A certain gentleman of the law, perceiving a very fine girl, which she was at that time, often in the walks, took the opportunity of conversing with her, and soon after persuaded her to come and make some tea for him in his chambers. The sequel, it were needless to relate: she was debauched, and soon after deserted by her betrayer. The consequence of which was, having lost her place, and being destitute of character, she was obliged to have recourse to her beauty for a subsistence. She took lodgings near Red Lyon Square, and had a number of successive admirers. She was, at this time, not about twenty; tall and well made, with a fine open expressive countenance, large amorous eyes; her other features in due symmetry; her mouth very agreeable, and her teeth regular; in a word, she was at that time one of the finest women upon the town, and, accordingly, made one of the best figures from the emoluments of her employments. She was some time after taken into keeping by a man of fortune, with whom she made a summer excursion into the country; but, upon his demise, her finances being exhausted, she was compelled to have recourse to a more general commerce, in which she has not been so successful, as before; and chagrin added to the usual irregularities accidental to her profession, has diminished those charms which were before so attracting; her face is now rather bloated, and she is grown somewhat masculine in her person; she may, nevertheless, still be pronounced a very good piece, and a desirable woman.'

The records of the Foundling Hospital in London, which was Britain's first children's charity, attest to how many women found themselves deserted by seducers. Prior to this the only provision for abandoned children was Christ's hospital, founded in 1552, but by 1676 illegitimate children were no longer admitted there. After this the only provision for illegitimate babies was parish poorhouses or the workhouse; during the 1720s and 1730s, the death rate for children in workhouses was over ninety per cent. It was not just the illegitimate who suffered for the poor who fell on hard times were also subject to the nightmare of the workhouse. The eighteenth century saw what artist William Hogarth described as 'a golden age of English philanthropy' and the Foundling Hospital was a beneficiary of that philanthropic zeal. Indeed he himself had a long association with the Hospital and decorated the walls of it with donated pieces of his own art, as well as that of other sympathetic artists.

The moral censure that accompanied any dealings with the Foundling Hospital only added to the distress of being parted from your child. A frowning middle class panel at the Hospital decided whether the unmarried mothers were of good character and passed judgement on whether the Hospital would take in their illegitimate babies. On 25 March 1741, a temporary house in Hatton Garden was the base for the new hospital and that night the first children were admitted. It is said that heart-wrenching cries were heard throughout the night as mothers were parted from their children. The tokens that mothers left with the babies to remind them of their love are truly heartbreaking. In these small coins, ribbons and notes, you can see the hope that remained that they would meet again, however unlikely it was to be.

One note, pinned to the clothing of little Florella Burley, born 19 June 1758, read 'Pray let particular care be taken of this little child' while one heart-shaped, silver-coloured token was engraved with 'You have my heart, though we must part'. Some of the tokens were hearts split in two, the hope being that the mother could return one day and identify her child by the heart half she had left with him.

The lower down the social scale you were, the fewer options were available to you for dealing with the consequences of sex before marriage. As such, some employers stipulated that servants were to have 'no followers' so as to ensure propriety and also, to some extent, protect their female employees from the evils of seduction, although it is as well to say that most servants who were sexually assaulted were the victims of their masters or male relatives of their employers. Where a master was not a rapist, you could still suffer a terrible fate if caught stealing. Once a servant was tarnished with that reputation, no domestic work would again be possible and many women were forced to turn to prostitution. Shockingly, G.P. Merrick, chaplain of London's Millbank Prison, writing in 1890 found that out of 16,000 prostitutes he interviewed, forty per cent had been domestic servants.

However, Charles Dickens in his *Dickens's Dictionary of London* (1879) advised against employers attempting to govern the romances of their staff. 'A serious mistake, and one too often made, is to lay down the hard–and–fast rule "no followers allowed". Servants always have had and always will have followers, whether their masters and mistresses like it or no. It is much wiser to recognise this fact, and to authorise the visits of the "follower" at proper times and seasons, first taking pains to ascertain that his antecedents and character are good.'

Young men had considerably more power to engage in sexual activity with far fewer consequences, unless the woman in question had violent male relations who decided to force the issue of marriage. Respectable young men often came to the marriage bed virgins, but more worldly ones had often already engaged in relations with the ladies of the night. Samuel Beeton, who was keen on writing authoritative etiquette advice for ladies and gentlemen in the nineteenth century, may well have infected his wife, Isabella, with syphilis due to a visit to a brothel prior to his marriage – as convincingly argued by historian Kathryn Hughes.

Sex was not considered to be a male problem, it was the 'wages of sin' in the form of illegitimate children that was frowned upon. Plus the perpetual bachelor became a figure of fun and somewhat despised by a society that placed marriage high on the list of responsibilities of an adult male. While historically, from the Roman Empire onwards, many western countries have attempted to impose a 'bachelor tax' (Britain repealed its Marriage Duty Act in 1706 when it appeared not to have had much effect on the behaviour of single men), it is more the cultural gibes that continued unabated. For example in his novel *Le Cousin Pons* (1847), Honoré de Balzac describes the main character thus: 'Like all confirmed bachelors, who hold their own lodgings in horror, and live as much as possible in other people's houses, Pons was accustomed to the formulas and facial contortions which do duty for feeling in the world…' Pons is shown humiliating himself by running small errands for the families he dines with in order to continue living off their tables. It is telling that the original title of the book was 'Le Parasite'. Honour and duty demanded that a man marry and run his own household.

In 1740 the original version of *Beauty and the Beast* by Gabrielle de Villeneuve was published in France. It is interesting to note that the beast in this version only turned back into the prince after, not before, the wedding night. This seems to be an allegory for the idea that men are savage creatures and only sex within marriage can tame their 'beastly' libido.

However, society had the perfect weapon against licentious behaviour: the chaperon.

Chapter Five

In Praise of Chaperons

*Many a reputation has been saved by a handy sibling
or great-aunt in tow*

'A young lady, during her first winter in society, does not use a separate visiting card, but has her name engraved on that of her mother or chaperon', declared *The Home Manual* in 1889. Written by Mrs John A Logan, this guide to all things domestic was unequivocal in stressing the importance of ensuring that you had a chaperon to police your first season 'out' in society. A chaperon could be any older, married or widowed woman such as a sister or an aunt or even an unrelated family friend. Of course the chaperon had to have an impeccable reputation herself. While not considered as appropriate in society, within a domestic setting, siblings could also be chaperons to ensure that nothing untoward occurred between a couple. The high number of working class brides who came to the altar pregnant indicates sex before marriage was not seen as such a terrible sin, since it proved that the woman was capable of conceiving. However, by the start of the Regency era such lax attitudes had been properly nipped in the bud and much more was being done to protect the offspring of the well-to-do.

G. M. Woodward's cartoon, showing the futility of mothers advising daughters who are in love, was published c.1790–1801. (*Public domain*)

Servants often doubled as impromptu, unofficial chaperons. For one thing, they were known to gossip and sending a servant out of the room when meeting with a gentleman caller could raise eyebrows. They could also bear vital witness should a man think he were being cuckolded. The case of Lady Colin Campbell's divorce hinged on evidence from servants watching her allegedly having sex with her lover through a keyhole. However, the nobility realised that a more effective ploy would be to have a strata between themselves and their lower class servants, in the form of nannies and governesses.

Joanna Martin in her book *Wives and Daughters* (2004), reveals that professional nannies were a Victorian invention designed to counter the effects of children spending too much time in the company of servants.

'Some households employed two such women: In 1806 Mary Talbot wrote that she would like to have two governesses at Penrice, so that the sub-governess could supervise the children when the superior governess was otherwise occupied "to prevent their ever being with servants".

'Within the household, the governess occupied a position that was uneasily poised between the family and the servants, and it was inevitable that she should suffer from the anomalies of her situation. A governess had to be a lady and, while socially inferior to her employers, she would invariably consider herself to be superior to the main body of servants.'

This role extended until the governess herself married or, if she remained with the family, to the coming of age of her charges, wherein her duties would often become those of a companion and chaperon.

On occasion, however, even the governess proved a dangerous temptation for the master of the house. In Jennifer Newby's *Women's Lives* (2011), we learn of the scandal caused by governesses who married 'above themselves'.

A humorous 1897 photographic print on curved stereo card entitled 'Partiality' showing a pouting chaperon, possibly a sibling, enviously looking at a beau making his 'partiality' known. (*Boston Public Library*)

'The 1861 census reveals that there were 24,700 governesses in England and Wales. These women earned very little, most between £35 and £80 a year from 1830 to 1890. As well as earning a servant-sized salary, governesses had to put up with being 'higher class' than their fellow servants in the household, but never the social equal of their employers. In 1858, a woman journalist wrote scathingly:

'Just let a remote idea be entertained of marriage between a son, or any other member of the family, and the governess; why, another siege of Troy would scarcely occasion more commotion – the anger, scorn, vituperation lavished on the artful creature.'

However, while working for a 'particularly attentive and affectionate' widower, 19-year-old May Pinhorn was surprised when "He got me into a summer house and told me he hoped I would be his wife, an offer I promptly and brutally refused."'

The story of one of the daughters of the Fox Strangways family at the centre of Joanna Martin's *Wives and Daughters: Women and Children in the Georgian Country House* (2004) shows that, even with the provision of governesses, love will out.

The daughter of Lord Illchester, Susan Fox Strangways, eloped in 1764 with an actor named William O'Brien, whom she had met at an amateur theatrical performance in which Susan was appearing. Her elopement was made possible while she was visiting a friend and able to send the household servants away. To marry an actor was unheard of for an Earl's daughter at the time, and Horace Walpole wrote to his friend Horace Mann, the British Resident in Florence, about it:

'A melancholy affair has happened to Lord Illchester. His eldest daughter, Lady Susan, a very pleasing girl though not handsome, married herself two days ago at Covent Garden church to O'Brien, a handsome young actor. Lord Illchester doted on her and was the most indulgent of fathers. 'Tis a cruel blow.' The couple were promptly shipped off to America in the hope that they would find their fortune there.'

While her chaperon sleeps a young girl keeps watch on her as her lover on bended knee kisses her hand. A mid–nineteenth century engraving by H.C. Shenton after F.P.Stephanoff. (*Wellcome Library, London*)

An older woman acts as chaperon to a girl who is being courted by a young man. (*Wellcome Library, London*)

Not all chaperons met with such failure, it has to be said. The American etiquette author, Emily Post, still displayed a Victorian adherence to the usefulness of chaperons when writing in 1922.

'As a matter of fact the only young girl who is really "free," is she whose chaperon is never very far away. She need give conventionality very little thought, and not bother about her P's and Q's at all, because her chaperon is always a strong and protective defense; but a young girl who is unprotected by a chaperon is in the position precisely of an unarmed traveler walking alone among wolves—his only defense is in not attracting their notice.'

In Elizabeth Gaskell's 1855 novel *North and South*, the hero John Thornton spots Margaret Hale at a late hour of the night with a gentleman and no chaperon. The unknown man turns out to be her brother, but Thornton naturally assumes that he is her lover. The company of a chaperon also meant that any gentleman in your party was rendered safe from speculation.

Generally, it was acknowledged by most that the presence of a chaperon was not necessarily an absolute protection against mischief, but the sight of one let the world know that you knew what was proper in polite society. Emily Post again:

'Ethically the only chaperon is the young girl's own sense of dignity and pride; she who has the right attributes of character needs no chaperon – ever. If she is wanting in decency and proper pride, not even Argus could watch over her! But apart from ethics, there are the conventions to think of, and the conventions of propriety demand that every young woman must be protected by a chaperon, because otherwise she will be misjudged.'

If an unsuitable man attempted to make an acquaintance with her charge, Emily Post urged a chaperon to ensure that this did not come to pass.

'If an objectionable person – meaning one who can not be considered a gentleman – is inclined to show the young girl attentions, it is of course her duty to cut the acquaintance short at the beginning before the young girl's interest has become aroused. For just such a contingency as this it is of vital importance that confidence and sympathy exist between the chaperon and her charge.'

Adam Petrie, in his *Rules of Good Deportment and of Good Breeding* (1720), writes:

HIDE AND SEEK.

Entitled 'Hide and seek' this 1896 print shows a couple hiding from the girl's frantically searching chaperon. (*Public domain*)

'If a young man and a young woman be in a room and you be to remove from them, and if there is none with them, it is imprudent and uncivil to shut the door after you; for if a person of a narrow soul shall come and find them shut up in a room they may be ready to stain their reputation, which should be dear unto us and cautiously preserved.'

Samuel Beeton, in his *Complete Etiquette for Ladies* (1876), advises a young woman to explicitly ask for advice as to whether a man is suitable or not.

'If a gentleman gives you reason to believe that he wishes to engage your affections, seek the advice of your parents, that they may gain for you every necessary particular with regard to his morals and disposition, and means of suitably providing for you.'

One can't imagine that many young ladies paused in the pursuit of passion to consider asking their parents to investigate the suitability of a prospective beau.

A chaperon's duties could be arduous. Emily Post writes of what she should expect if her young charge is hosting friends at a party or is receiving guests:

'The chaperon (or a parent) should never go to bed until the last young man has left the house. It is an unforgivable breach of decorum to allow a young girl to sit up late at night with a young man – or a number of them. On returning home from a party, she must not invite or allow a man to "come in for a while." Even her fiancé must bid her good night at the door if the hour is late, and someone ought always to sit up, or get up, to let her in. No young girl ought to let herself in with a latch-key. In old-fashioned days no lady had a latch-key. And it is still fitting and proper for a servant to open the door for her.'

Ms Post also gives a startling example of regional ideas of propriety. 'Even in Victorian days it was proper in Baltimore for a young girl to go to the theater alone with a man, and to have him see her home from a ball was not only permitted but absolutely correct.'

Of course there were dire consequences to having a less than zealous chaperon. As such, most chaperons were from the couple's immediate family or highly trusted governesses with a longstanding connection to the family.

Chapter Six

Love Songs, Letters, and Poems

Articulating your desire can get you an assignation – or potentially an execution!

Very few people, perhaps as little as five per cent, were able to read and write in fifteenth century Britain. In fact, it was the late Victorian era before free elementary education was introduced in Britain, allowing the majority of the populace to become literate. So initially wooing by letter was a luxury only enjoyed by the educated. However, the use of the spoken word in the form of romantic ballads and poetry was accessible to all.

As any successful lover knows, words are crucial to seduction. Whether a poem is recited or a letter is read, no wooing can be done without the liberal use of tender sentiments expressed correctly. This places the tongue-tied or silent lover at a distinct disadvantage.

Thankfully, the era in which we begin our journey into romantic words of courtship had a code in place to ensure that every man knew what was expected of him when wooing.

The medieval poem *The Romance of the Rose* – begun by Guillaume de Lorris in 1237 and finished forty years later by Jean de Meung – is a work of courtly literature, which served to educate people about the edicts of courtly love. This was supplemented by the medieval tradition of troubadours at court, whose music expounded the joys of courtly love, chivalry and courtesy.

They were the renowned poets of love who performed music and poetry in the High Middle Ages (c.1100-1350) and many came from the southern half of France, northern Spain and parts of Italy. Karen Ralls explains in *Medieval Mysteries* (2014) how the songs of the troubadour and trobairitz (female troubadour) were grouped into three major styles: *trobar leu* (light), *trobar ric* (rich) and *trobar clus* (closed). *Trobar leu* was the most popular form as the words were the most simple and could be understood most generally, while both *ric* and *clus* used symbolic and metaphoric language that would only have been accessible to a few in the know. This is in addition to the different 'schools' within the tradition. Ralls writes of the origin of troubadour poems:

> 'The earliest troubadour whose work has survived is Guilhem de Peitieus, better known as Duke William IX of Aquitaine, who lived in the late eleventh and early twelfth centuries. The medieval work *Orderic Vitalis* refers to William composing songs about his experiences on his return from a crusade in 1102, with some experts claiming this may be the earliest reference to troubadour lyrics known today.'

William IX's wife, Philippa of Toulouse, might well have wished that he hadn't been quite so interested in romance since she was usurped by the Viscountess Dangerosa, an affair for which the Duke was excommunicated from the Church although they termed it an abduction. When a papal representative who was bald asked the Duke to return the Viscountess to her husband, William responded "Curls will grow on your pate before I part with the Viscountess". Poor Philippa retired to an abbey and passed away two years later.

His song, *Farai Chansoneta Nueva*, or 'I Shall Write A New Song' showed the typical yearnings that were the meat and wine of courtly expression. Here's an effusive extract from that poem:

A medieval lover is pulled up in a basket to speak with his beloved. From the German illuminated manuscript, *Codex Manesse*, which features the work of many famous poets and was produced between 1305 and 1315. (*Public domain*)

Her skin is white as ivory;
No other's in my history:
An urgent show of love for me
Is needed to remove all doubt.
I'll die now, by St. Gregory,
Without a kiss, indoors or out.
What good, fair lady, will be done
If with your love you'd up and run?

Perhaps you want to be a nun?
I tell you now, that I love you:
By sorrow I will be undone
Unless my claim appeals to you.

(Translated by James H. Donalson)

Troubadours were responsible for composing some of the most popular love songs of the age and the taste for these flowed from the European courts down to the rest of society, although the songs became more rustic in nature when they drifted far away from the refined sensibilities of court.

'Maiden in the Moor' is an example of an eleventh century troubadour composition that is still sung as a folk song today. While not explicitly referring to love, the song has a great deal of romantic imagery and symbolism from the Middle Ages, such as the primrose and violets that was her 'mete' (sustenance or food) and her dwelling or 'bour' was among the red rose and the lily-flower. These floral evocations indicate the ideas of purity that surrounded the ballads of this era. It was so successful at conveying those ideas that the Church later attempted to co-opt the song's melody and turn it into an altogether more ecclesiastical offering.

Here are the lyrics of the full song:

'Maiden in the Moor Lay'

Maiden in the moor lay –
In the moor lay –
Seven-night fulle,
Seven-night fulle,
Maiden in the moor lay –
In the moor lay–
Seven-nights fulle and a day.

Well was her mete.
What was her mete?
The primerole and the–
Well was her mete.
What was her mete?
The primerole and the violette.

Well was her drinke.
What was her drinke?
The colde water of the–
The colde water of the–
Well was her drinke.
What was her drinke?
The colde water of the welle-spring.

Well was her bour.
What was her bour?
The rede rose and the–
The rede rose and the–
Well was her bour.
What was her bour?
The rede rose and the lily-flour.

Why was there such an emphasis on purity during this time? One theory about the reason this chaste tradition of courtly love swept the western world was that there was a surplus of 'second sons'. Only the eldest son inherited land and were attractive marriage prospects. Younger brothers were obliged to make their own way in the world and could only hope to marry into wealth. Born into the nobility yet without the means to marry, they would often join the crusades, embark on a career in the Church or spend time wooing wealthy women.

It was considered a safe outlet for these young men to woo with song and deed a lady they would never consummate their love with. The other great advantage to courtly love was that most marriages in this period were contracted for the purposes of alliances, property or other financial or political reasons. This provided a chance for a married woman to experience being wooed without any possible stain on her character or threat to her marriage.

Folk songs show how disastrous the result of consummating an adulterous love could be. One of the 305 traditional ballads collected by Francis James Child between 1882 and 1898 is the tale of 'Little Musgrave and Lady Barnard'. The tale itself predates the collection and has been traced back to the seventeenth century; in later versions, Little Musgrave is called Matty Groves. In the song a servant of Lord Donald (a name variant on Barnard) is spotted by the Lord's wife at church and is seduced by Lady Donald. Another retainer runs to tell Lord Donald who is away from home, who returns to find the lovers in bed.

Little Matty Groves, he lay down and took a little sleep
When he awoke, Lord Donald was standing at his feet
Saying "How do you like my feather bed and how do you like my
    sheets?
How do you like my lady who lies in your arms asleep?"
"Oh, well I like your feather bed and well I like your sheets
But better I like your lady gay who lies in my arms asleep"

"Well, get up, get up," Lord Donald cried, "get up as quick as you
  can
It'll never be said in fair England that I slew a naked man"
"Oh, I can't get up, I won't get up, I can't get up for my life
For you have two long beaten swords and I not a pocket knife"
"Well it's true I have two beaten swords and they cost me deep in
   the purse
But you will have the better of them and I will have the worse
And you will strike the very first blow and strike it like a man
I will strike the very next blow and I'll kill you if I can"

So Matty struck the very first blow and he hurt Lord Donald sore
Lord Donald struck the very next blow and Matty struck no more
And then Lord Donald, he took his wife and he sat her on his knee
Saying "Who do you like the best of us, Matty Groves or me?"
And then up spoke his own dear wife, never heard to speak so free
"I'd rather a kiss from dead Matty's lips than you or your finery"

Lord Donald he jumped up and loudly he did bawl
He struck his wife right through the heart and pinned her against
   the wall
"A grave, a grave," Lord Donald cried, "to put these lovers in
But bury my lady at the top for she was of noble kin"

Interestingly, the poignant idea of an adulterous wife preferring her
dead lover even as it seals her own fate may well have been the root of the
inaccurate rumour that Katherine Howard said at her execution that she
died a queen but would have preferred to live as Culpeper's wife.

Eternal love triangles

Duke William's granddaughter, Eleanor of Aquitaine, brought the tradition of courtly love over from the continent to England in 1154 when her second husband, Henry of Anjou, became King of England. Highly educated and a skilled politician, Eleanor was a great patron of the arts. The poets and writers of the courtly tradition appealed to her sensibilities, having always been forced to make political marriages rather than giving in to any notion of romantic love. Her daughter, Marie, brought these ideals and ideas to the court of Champagne of which she became countess and was patron to the troubadour Chrétien de Troyes. Tobias Churton writes in his book, *The Gnostic Philosophy* (2003):

> 'Courtly love became a part of courtly life and its customs and special forms came to dictate what was expected of a *courtier*, who was usually a knight of lower rank than the *signeur* who might, in this region (Champagne), be a woman. In the Languedoc, privileged women could enjoy the respect and indeed love expected from a vassal. The basic form of Fine Love is woven into this relationship of vassal to lord, hence the romantic custom of getting on one knee before the loved one ...'

Who would have thought that this is where the custom of kneeling to propose marriage to your beloved comes from? The strong women of this time and region, who would often be left in charge while their lords were off fighting in the Crusades, were being given the respect and submission usually offered to a lord by a vassal.

A famous example from this time is the story of Tristan and Isolde. Although based on an old Celtic tale, the story became popular in the twelfth century when many songs retold the legend. The *Prose Tristan* (c. 1240) by an unknown author or authors was the version upon which Sir Thomas Mallory based his tale of King Arthur, Guinevere and

Lancelot. Tristan, a nephew (or in some versions a mere courtier-knight) of King Mark of Cornwall, is sent to escort Isolde, Mark's fiancée, from Ireland to marry Mark. The couple have been betrothed in order to end a war between Ireland and Cornwall. Since the marriage is not one of love, Isolde is given a love potion by a kinswoman of hers, half of which she is instructed to take and the other half she is to give to Mark. However, she gives it to Tristan instead and the couple fall in love. The courtly versions of the story have the lovers consummate their love, but the potion excuses them from responsibility for the transgression. Elements of the courtly tradition exist in Tristan's regard for Mark,

Edmund Leighton's 1902 painting shows Tristan and Isolde with her husband, King Mark, in the background. (*Public domain*)

despite his betrayal, and in Mark's refusal to believe others in his court about the couple's adultery.

This legend is where the notion of impossible love enters the romantic milieu and it ties in well with the yearning without consummation that characterises courtly love. From this time onwards writers and artists find an attraction in the idea of tragic love.

Henry VIII, who is more notorious for his marital exploits than any other achievements during his reign, was a king whose wives often suffered in the cause of tragic love. Perhaps the most tragic of all is the story of Katherine Howard, the pretty first cousin of Anne Boleyn who was just 15 when she was betrothed to the 49-year old king. After marrying Henry in the summer of 1540, poor Katherine would be tried for treason and executed less than two years later in February 1542. Suspicions were raised about Katherine having had sexual relations with Francis Dereham prior to her marriage. An investigation was conducted and one of the main pieces of evidence against her was a letter she had written to Thomas Culpeper, a courtier in Henry's retinue. It was damning in that it contained phrases such as 'it makes my heart die to think what fortune I have that I cannot be always in your company'.

That might have been enough for a fiercely jealous, thin-skinned spouse such as Henry, but there was also testimony from the ladies who attended Katherine prior to her arrival at court that she had engaged in a serious dalliance with Francis Dereham and the two even went so far as to call each other 'husband' and 'wife'. Poor Katherine's fate was probably sealed when her closest servant Joan Bulmer revealed that the young queen had urged her to arrange a secret meeting with Culpeper. While Culpeper did not admit to consummating the affair, he admitted that the queen was 'languishing and dying for love of him', which would have been enough to hurt Henry's not inconsiderable ego. The mere intention to have an affair was treachery enough and the parties were to suffer for it.

In the end both Culpeper and Dereham were executed in December 1541 and their severed heads mounted on stakes atop London Bridge. Two months later, the young queen – stripped of her royal title by then – was taken by boat en route to her own execution, passing under the bridge on which she could see the decomposing heads of her former lovers.

Perhaps courtly love was a better option for potential lovers, since it was rare indeed for a love affair to end in dangerous sexual congress. Those espousing the virtues of what was described as 'fine love' were not overly concerned with sex alone – or at least pretended not to be. R. Barber in *The Knight and Chivalry* (2000) writes: 'Troubadour poetry is not about women, their beauty or charms; it is about the lover and his longings. The highest praise is measured in terms of the lady's influence on the admirer, and so the qualities of the love loom large in their philosophy.'

The written word was not always connected with the higher ideals of sexless romance, as the notable example of John Wilmot (1647-1680), the second Earl of Rochester, shows. The Earl's extremely saucy poems were apparently not for publication, but nevertheless scandalised later generations with their lewdness. Here's one dealing with premature ejaculation and subsequent impotence!

The Imperfect Enjoyment

Naked she lay, clasped in my longing arms,
I filled with love, and she all over charms;
Both equally inspired with eager fire,
Melting through kindness, flaming in desire.
With arms, legs, lips close clinging to embrace,
She clips me to her breast, and sucks me to her face.
Her nimble tongue, love's lesser lightning, played
Within my mouth, and to my thoughts conveyed
Swift orders that I should prepare to throw
The all-dissolving thunderbolt below.

My fluttering soul, sprung with the pointed kiss,
Hangs hovering o'er her balmy brinks of bliss.
But whilst her busy hand would guide that part
Which should convey my soul up to her heart,
In liquid raptures I dissolve all o'er,
Melt into sperm, and spend at every pore.
A touch from any part of her had done 't:
Her hand, her foot, her very look's a cunt.
Smiling, she chides in a kind murmuring noise,
And from her body wipes the clammy joys,
When, with a thousand kisses wandering o'er
My panting bosom, "Is there then no more?"
She cries. "All this to love and rapture's due;
Must we not pay a debt to pleasure too?"
But I, the most forlorn, lost man alive,
To show my wished obedience vainly strive:
I sigh, alas! and kiss, but cannot swive.
Eager desires confound my first intent,
Succeeding shame does more success prevent,
And rage at last confirms me impotent.
Ev'n her fair hand, which might bid heat return
To frozen age, and make cold hermits burn,
Applied to my dear cinder, warms no more
Than fire to ashes could past flames restore.
Trembling, confused, despairing, limber, dry,
A wishing, weak, unmoving lump I lie.
This dart of love, whose piercing point, oft tried,
With virgin blood ten thousand maids has dyed,
Which nature still directed with such art
That it through every cunt reached every heart—
Stiffly resolved, 'twould carelessly invade
Woman or man, nor ought its fury stayed:

Where'er it pierced, a cunt it found or made—
Now languid lies in this unhappy hour,
Shrunk up and sapless like a withered flower.
Thou treacherous, base deserter of my flame,
False to my passion, fatal to my fame,
Through what mistaken magic dost thou prove
So true to lewdness, so untrue to love?
What oyster-cinder-beggar-common whore
Didst thou e'er fail in all thy life before?
When vice, disease, and scandal lead the way,
With what officious haste doest thou obey!
Like a rude, roaring hector in the streets
Who scuffles, cuffs, and justles all he meets,
But if his king or country claim his aid,
The rakehell villain shrinks and hides his head;
Ev'n so thy brutal valor is displayed,
Breaks every stew, does each small whore invade,
But when great Love the onset does command,
Base recreant to thy prince, thou dar'st not stand.
Worst part of me, and henceforth hated most,
Through all the town a common fucking post,
On whom each whore relieves her tingling cunt
As hogs on gates do rub themselves and grunt,
Mayst thou to ravenous chancres be a prey,
Or in consuming weepings waste away;
May strangury and stone thy days attend;
May'st thou never piss, who didst refuse to spend
When all my joys did on false thee depend.
And may ten thousand abler pricks agree
To do the wronged Corinna right for thee.

This would not have been sent to a mistress, unless Rochester wanted to laugh at himself, which, by all counts, he was capable of doing. Much literature though was produced for the purposes of courting.

Poetry and songs are not the only ways to woo a lady, however, and history has many famous marriages contracted on the basis of letters

The Love Letter by Jean-Honoré Fragonard (1732–1806). (*Public domain*)

written during the courtship. More formal suitors would even make the offer of marriage via a letter rather than in person, perhaps hoping the pain of a potential rejection would sting less in written rather than verbal form.

Author ES Turner writes in *A History of Courting* (1954) of a wonderful anecdote in which a passionate proposal was reconsidered and retracted without the lady ever being aware of it.

'The Victorian Post Office was evidently not rigidly bound of regulations. There is a story that Theodore Hook wrote a letter containing a proposal of marriage, posted it and then changed his mind. Hurrying round to the post office he authenticated his writing and was handed back the fatal letter. Today any local postmaster

Victorian Valentine's cards were so romantic that the tradition continues to this day. Cards from 1899. (*Public domain*)

would rather doom a couple to an unhappy marriage than disgorge a proposal once entrusted to his care.'

Passion was generally frowned upon by the Victorians, but they did ensure, by introducing the penny post in 1840, that expressions of desire could have an easy outlet. Books offering gentlemen advice on writing letters for various purposes began to appear, although at times these served more as amusing guides of what not to do.

The Gentleman's Letter Writer was published at the turn of the century and, in the tradition of Victorian self-improvement manuals, it explicitly condemned attempting to engage a lady acquaintance through the post. Such vulgar behaviour towards a lady to whom the correspondent had not been introduced was deemed utterly reprehensible. The editors were also amused at some of the profuse declarations of love gentlemen writers had had cause to set down on paper, so much so that they re-published them – whether to inspire other correspondents to such flights of fancy or to discourage them from it, is not entirely clear.

Here is an example of a particular bit of purple prose that appeared in that book.

Letter to a Lady

Dear Madam, I have been so harassed with love, doubt, distraction, and a thousand other wild and nameless feelings, since I had the happiness of being in your company, that I have been unable to form one sane reflection, or to separate events from the feelings that accompanied them – in fact, I have been totally unable to bring my thoughts into anything like regularity, for they are so entirely mixed up with the idea of yourself, that the business of this world, and the pursuits of amusement and pleasure, have been entirely forgotten in the one passion that holds undivided empire over my soul.

I have deferred from day to day penning this confession to you, in order that I might have been enabled to have done so with some degree of ease and calmness; but the hope has proved fruitless. I can resist no longer, for to keep silent on a subject which is interwoven with my very existence, would be death to me. No, I am unable to do so, and I have therefore determined to lay open to you the sufferings of my heart, and to implore from you a restoration of that peace and happiness which once were mine.

You, my dear Miss –, are alone the cause of my unhappiness, and to you alone can I look for a fervent passion that devours my soul for your adorable self, can only be allayed by the declaration that I am loved as fervently in return. But dare I ask so much purity, so much sweetness, mildness and modesty, to make such a declaration? – I know not what I say – but O! my dear Miss –, be merciful, and if you cannot love me – say, at least, that you do not hate me.

Never could I survive the idea of being hateful to that angelic being, whose love I prize more than existence itself. Let me then cling to the idea that time may accomplish that which, I fain hope, a first impression has done resuming, unless a fatal pre-engagement exists (a thing I dare not trust myself to think of), that you comply with my request, seeing that my designs are perfectly sincere and honourable. I remain, waiting with utmost impatience for your favourable reply.

Dear Miss –, Your devoted servant till death.

In contrast, the suggested letter to the father of the object of one's affection is considerably briefer:

From a Lover to a Father on his attachment to the Daughter

Sir, – As I scorn to act in any manner that may bring reproach upon myself and family, and hold clandestine proceedings unbecoming in any man of character, I take the liberty of distinctly avowing my love for your

daughter, and humbly request your permission to pay her my addresses,
as I flatter myself my family and expectances will be found not unworthy
of your notice. I have some reason to imagine, that I am not altogether
disagreeable to your daughter; but I assure you, honestly, that I have not
as yet endeavoured to win her affections, for fear it might be repugnant
to a father's will.

I am, Sir,
Your most obedient servant.

The writers don't leave the poor father in the lurch as to how to reply
to such a request, offering both negative and affirmative templates for
responses:

The Father's answer in the negative

Sir, — I make no doubt of the truth of your assertions, relative to yourself,
character, and connections; but as I think my daughter too young to
enter into such a serious engagement, I request I may hear no more of
your passion for the present; in every other respect, I am, Sir, Your most
obedient.

The Father's answer in the affirmative

Sir, — There is so much candour and honour apparent in your letter, that
to withhold my consent would be both ungenerous and unjust. As the duty
of a father demands, I shall first make some necessary inquiries, assuring
you that I would never oppose my daughter's choice, except I had some
very just reason to imagine it would be productive of ill consequences,
for I am convinced that, in the marriage state, happiness consists only in
reciprocal affection. You may therefore depend upon hearing from me in
a few days; till then, I remain, Your very faithful servant.

From these pedestrian and socially sanctioned exaltations, we move on to the truly witty and flirtatious. Courtesans were great at written repartee and found many new suitors through this method. Perhaps one of the most famous is Harriette Wilson (1786–1845) whose audacity won her the attentions of many rich and powerful benefactors. She wrote to the Prince of Wales saying that she was told that she is 'very beautiful' and perhaps he would like to see her. When he wrote back agreeing to a meeting and asking her to visit him, she sent the following cheeky response:

Sir, to travel fifty-two miles, in this bad weather merely to see a man with only the given number of legs, arms, fingers &c. would, you must admit, be madness in a girl like myself surrounded by humble admirers who are ever ready to travel any distance for the honour of kissing the tip of her little finger; but, if you can prove to me that you are one bit better than any man who may be ready to attend my bidding, I'll e'en start for London directly. So, if you can do anything better, in the way of pleasing a lady, than ordinary men, write directly: if not, adieu, Monsieur le Prince.

I won't say Yours

By day or night or any kind of light

Because you are too impudent

Courtesans knew that the way to seduce a man was to tease and even insult in the first instance to increase desire in a man. Regency life was very mannered and the respectable women that these men came into contact with on a daily basis would be a distinct contrast to the witty, flirty communications they could expect from a courtesan. This was as true in earlier times too as this letter on love and seduction by Ninon de L'Enclos (1616-1706) shows; she was the beautiful courtesan whose salons attracted writers such as Moliere and Fontenelle.

Here she saucily encourages the Marquis de Sevigné to lie for the purposes of seduction.

Ninon de L'Enclos to the Marquis de Sevigné

Shall I tell you what renders love dangerous?

It is the sublime idea which one often appears to have about it. But in exact truth, Love, taken as a passion, is only a blind instinct which one must know how to value correctly; an appetite which determines you for one object rather than for another, without being able to give any reason for one's preference; considered as a link of friendship, when reason presides over it, it is not a passion, it is no longer love, it is an affectionate esteem, in truth, but peaceful, incapable of leading you out of bounds; when, however, you walk in the traces of our ancient heroes of romance, you go in for the grand sentiments, you will see that this pretended heroism only makes of love a deplorable and often disastrous folly. It is a true fanaticism; but if you strip it of all those virtues of hearsay, it will soon minister to your happiness and to your pleasures.

Believe me, that if it were reason or enthusiasm which governed affairs of the heart, love would become either insipid or a delirium. The only way to avoid these two extremes is to follow the path I indicate to you. You have need of being amused and you will only find what you require for that amongst the women I speak of. Your heart needs occupation; they are made to captivate it ...

Honesty in love, marquis! How can you think of that! Ah, you are a good man gone wrong. I shall take great care not to show your letter; you would be dishonoured. You could not, you say, take on yourself to employ the manoeuvre which I have counselled you. Your frankness, your grandiose sentiments would have made your fortune in the old days. Then one used to treat love as a matter of honour; but today, when the corruption of the century has changed everything, Love is no more than a play of whim and vanity ... How many occasions do you not find where a lover gains as much by dissimulating the excess of his passion, as he would in others, by displaying greater passion than he feels?

Words to woo

While many accomplished writers penned moving love letters, there was often as much beauty in the communications of normal folk. We've already seen the wonderful example of true lover's knots, the folk art of the Pennsylvanian Quakers in the United States in the eighteenth and early nineteenth centuries.

However, another American tradition that was even handier during courtship was the mid to late nineteenth century tradition of confession albums, thought to originate in Victorian parlour games and fortune-telling amusements. More involved than autograph books, a lady might ask a gentleman caller to fill out her confession book (a later version used by American teenagers in the 1980s were known as 'slam books'). These were originally handwritten questions and later included pre-printed questions. Asking what your ideal partner would be like was a popular question to get some insight into your beau's true feelings.

Even Karl Marx's daughter, Jenny, kept a book with entries from 1865–1870, in which even her father's answers were recorded. Due to the fact that the practice was widespread among the middle classes and all the family and visiting guests filled them in, it was perceived as a fairly harmless way to flirt and was taken up with great enthusiasm.

AA Milne, writing in 1921, dates the end of the custom as being at the turn of the century. 'The confession-book, I suppose, has disappeared. It is

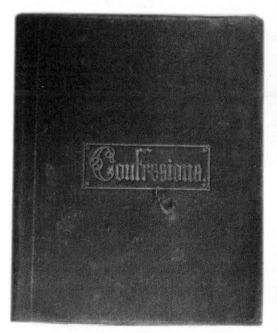

A cover of a confessions book by N. P Holmes
(*Licensed under CC BY-SA 3.0 via Wiki Commons*)

twenty years since I have seen one. As a boy I told some inquisitive owner what was my favourite food (porridge, I fancy), my favourite hero in real life and in fiction, my favourite virtue in woman, and so forth.'

Poems were also a popular way of stating one's feelings and there were plenty of poets whose work you could quote from if you weren't quite up to the job of writing one yourself. Perhaps the most famous love poem is the 'Roses are Red' stanza, a child's nursery rhyme dating from 1784, although the imagery of roses red and violets blue predate this by almost 200 years.

> *The rose is red, the violet's blue,*
> *The honey's sweet, and so are you.*
> *Thou are my love and I am thine;*
> *I drew thee to my Valentine:*
> *The lot was cast and then I drew,*
> *And Fortune said it should be you.*

If words win over your beloved, then your journey into successful wooing is only just beginning! Some believe that marriage is the start rather than the end of courtship, as we shall see in the next chapter.

Chapter Seven

How to be a Good Life Partner

Once you've said your vows, your work is only just beginning

A new husband carries his bride over the threshold of their new home so that she doesn't stumble and incur a bad omen. As the bride will soon discover, there are many other obstacles throughout marital life that she must avoid tripping over.

An image of family bliss from Mrs LG Abell's *Gems by the Wayside: An Offering of Purity and Truth*, 1878. (*Public domain*)

A humorous illustration in a 1902 edition of *Puck* magazine has a young woman suggesting that a man always has a companion to share his troubles with in marriage. The bachelor quips that not every man can afford a valet and butler. (*Public domain*)

Historically women left their father's home to enter that of their new husband, where his will was paramount. Women had no property rights until the late Victorian era and so everything she brought to the marriage was then the property of her husband, as indeed, to all intents and purposes, was she. This did not mean that she was not expected to fulfil her duties as a wife. Along with figuring out how to get along with a new husband, the new bride had to also move from being a dependent to the mistress of her own home. These new responsibilities often hung heavy on young shoulders.

For a young man, marriage meant the start of adult life and the prospect of sex sanctioned by the church and society at large. In 1754, Josiah Wedgwood – who was due to marry two days later – wrote blissfully of the day 'when she will reward all my faithful services and take me to her arms! To her nuptial bed! To pleasures which I am yet ignorant of.'

Yet, most women were as concerned about the practical realities of looking after a home as they were by the pleasures of the nuptial bed.

Financial matters

Juno Moneta, the Roman goddess from which the word 'money' derives, is also the patron of affianced couples about to marry. She protects funds and so in ancient Rome money was coined in her temple and the modern words 'money' and 'mint' derive from the Moneta part of her name. That she is patron of engaged couples indicates how important finances were considered to be within a marriage. Add to this the fact that much commerce in the past was conducted on credit with tradesmen whose accounts were settled quarterly or yearly. A woman's reputation as a good housekeeper was often key to her husband's standing in society.

On 1 August 1780, the Dublin-based *Saunders* newsletter carried an advertisement from M. Larkin, a disgruntled husband.

'An Imprudent Wife. Whereas Mary Larkin, (otherwise Paine) my wife, has behaved in a disorderly manner, which has made it necessary for me to caution the public against giving her any credit on my account, as I will not pay any debts contracted by her from this date. Given under my hand this 28th July 1780.'

While not all wives behaved 'in a disorderly manner', most did have to learn to budget and run the house, managing the household staff if they were lucky enough to have servants. A considerable portion of Mrs Beeton's famous *Book of Household Management* (1861) describes how to manage the various members of your staff. This was perhaps a strange preoccupation given that Isabella Beeton did not possess the luxury of a large house filled with staff at any point in her own life.

Beyond finances, there were several other areas in which a new wife could encounter conflict in her married life, even politics. As previously mentioned, patching was a beauty staple for both men and women in the sixteenth and seventeenth centuries, but it also had a political connotation. Those supporting the Tories would wear a patch on the left cheek, while fervent admirers of the Whigs would do so on the right. Women who adhered to this fashion often requested before marriage that

a Whole Lot, containing two Hundred Pounds.

AN IMPRUDENT WIFE.

WHEREAS Mary Larkin, (otherwise Paine) my Wife, has behaved in a disorderly Manner, which has made it necessary for me to caution the Public against giving her any Credit on my Account, as I will not pay any Debts contracted by her from this Date. Given under my Hand this 28th July, 1780.

M. LARKIN

The following Medicines are selling at James Potts's,

Saunders newsletter showing the advert placed in 1780 by a disgruntled husband. (*Public domain*)

This American print from 1912 shows that men continued to attempt to keep women away from politics and public life. (*Library of Congress*)

MARRIAGE OF THE BARONESS BURDETT-COUTTS WITH MR. W. ASHMEAD-BARTLETT.
[SEE "LIFE AND MARRIAGE OF LADY BURDETT-COUTTS."]

Sixty-seven-year-old Baroness Burdett-Coutts shocked polite society by marrying her 29-year-old secretary and thereby forfeiting three-fifths of her fortune. (*Public domain*) they be permitted to patch as per their conscience after marriage, if their husband happened to be of the opposite political persuasion.

Religion could also cause serious divisions too, especially in Tudor times when the establishment of the Church of England divided families – and often spouses – against each other. Whatever your particular sect, Christian teaching held that 'believing wives' had a duty to persuade 'unbelieving husbands' to pay heed to the Gospel. This was somewhat at odds with the general view that the ideal wife should be submissive and silent.

Samuel Beeton allows for that, first counselling women to not marry irreligious men and then advising them to ensure they adapt to their spouse's personality and needs.

> 'Women in this matter have no choice but that of accepting or rejecting offers made to them, but to compensate for this they have far greater powers of adaptation than men have. They can more easily conform themselves to circumstances and to the characters of their husbands than the husband can adapt his to his wife's.
>
> 'We call this a compensation for the want of choice they have, and so it is, but it makes a wife's responsibilities greater, for she is the more to blame for estrangement if either, after marriage, finds the disposition and tastes of the other different from what was expected. Any close observer will perceive that the happiest and most united marriages are not those where there is the greatest similarity of disposition, but those where, while each character has some traits in which the other is lacking, the wife has the good sense to put in practice this faculty of adapting herself to her husband's peculiarities of mind and taste.'

So, having accommodated her husband's 'peculiarities' the young wife would take over the running of her household. For many, particularly those who married as an alliance rather than for love, the courting period began after the wedding and not before. Getting to know your spouse was a difficult enterprise when the first year of marriage was a series of engagements where you were expected to attend together, but did not necessarily get to spend much time alone together. Culture also dictated that the man who was overly in love with his wife was despised and mocked as being 'under the thumb'. Victorian ladies were often impressed if a husband was kind enough to notice his wife after marriage, let alone woo her. Several of the self-help manuals that were the vogue at this time counsel women to be an unobtrusive and obedient helpmate to their husbands.

Author C.S. Lewis (1898-1963) had the idea that a husband was the head of his wife in the manner that Christ was head of the Church. He wrote, somewhat patronisingly, in *The Four Loves* (1960):

'This headship, then, is most fully embodied not in the husband we should all wish to be but in him whose marriage is most like a crucifixion; whose wife receives most and gives least, is most unworthy of him, is – in her own mere nature – least lovable. For the Church has not beauty but what the Bridegroom gives her; he does not find, but makes her, lovely. The chrism of this terrible coronation is to be seen not in the joys of any man's marriage but in its sorrows, in the sickness and sufferings of a good wife or the faults of a bad one, in his unwearying (never paraded) care or his inexhaustible forgiveness: forgiveness, not acquiescence. As Christ sees in the flawed, proud, fanatical or lukewarm Church on earth that Bride who will one day be without spot or wrinkle, and labours to produce the latter, so the husband whose headship is Christ-like (and he is allowed no other sort) never despairs. He is a King Cophetua who after twenty years still hopes that the beggar-girl will one day learn to speak the truth and wash behind her ears.'

The MAN-MIDWIFE, or FEMALE DELICACY after MARRIAGE:
Addressed to Husbands.
Published as the Act directs, 1st May 1773, by J. Hooper N.° 25. Ludgate hill.

A male-midwife suggestively examines an attractive pregnant woman, her disgruntled husband is led out of the room by a servant. Line engraving, 1773. (*Wellcome Library, London*)

Samuel Smiles, the author of the first such manual, entitled *Self-Help: With Illustrations of Character and Conduct* (1859), gave the example of Ann Denman as the ideal wife, because she sacrificed everything – including her own work as an artist – for the sake of her sculptor husband John Flaxman's career. Denman spent five years saving for Flaxman's trip to Rome where he was to study and illustrate, to counter her fear that people would think he had left off his best work upon marriage to her.

Poor wives also had significant sacrifices to make, even if they were sometimes symbolic. In seafaring communities, wives took care not to wash clothes on the days when their husbands set sail, in case through sympathetic magic their ships washed away in a storm. The women of Hallsands, in Devon, were said to wade out to sea with their fishermen husbands on their backs so that the men's feet would not get wet before their day's work.

What of husbands? What did they sacrifice upon achieving the marital state? Apart from the usual requirement to provide an income, perversely one of the best ways of a being a good husband was to avoid infecting your wife with syphilis. The wonderful biography of Mrs Beeton by Kathryn Hughes, *The Short Life and Long Times of Mrs Beeton* (2006) posits the idea that Mrs Beeton's demise was hastened by contracting syphilis from her husband, who may have visited prostitutes in his bachelor days.

Syphilis wasn't just a concern for Victorians. As far back as the 1490s, the disease swept across Europe, causing agonising deaths and disfigurements among its victims. The fact that syphilis was spread by men visiting prostitutes was soon common knowledge. Husbands would then spread the disease to their wives, to whom they also owed the 'marriage debt'. It prompted the Edinburgh council to issue an edict closing brothels in the town in 1497.

That men were aware of the potential dangers of visiting prostitutes is shown in *Harris's List of Covent Garden Ladies*, an eighteenth century 'gentleman's guide' to London's ladies of the night, which includes the following, rather impressively hypocritical, entry about a Miss Young:

Hieronymus Fracastorius (Girolamo Fracastoro) shows the shepherd Syphilus and the hunter Ilceus being warned against yielding to temptation with the danger of infection with syphilis. Engraving by Jan Sadeler I after Christoph Schwartz, 1588/1595. (*Wellcome Library, London*)

'She has very lately had the folly and wickedness to leave a certain hospital, before the cure of a certain distemper which she had was completed, and has thrown her contaminated carcass on the town again, for which we hold her inexcusable, and which was our only reason for repeating her name, that her company might be avoided, and that she might be held in the infamous light she so justly deserves for her wilful villainy.'

Fleet marriages

In the fifteenth and sixteenth centuries, there were few sex workers in rural communities. In any case, pre-marital sex was common, encouraged by the practice of handfasting. A 'hand-in-fist' betrothal as handfasting was called then was a form of trial marriage for a year and a day, in which both parties were able to decide whether or not they were suited to each other before committing to a formal marriage in front of a priest. In fact there were no state records of marriages at all before the mid-eighteenth century when Hardwicke's Marriage Act (1753) came into effect.

The Act required banns to be called on three successive Sundays before marriage and was designed to put an end to the scandal of Fleet marriages. These were marriages conducted by disreputable clergymen (some defrocked) in Fleet prison or its environs and were often touted for – a sort of early Las Vegas, with drunken sailors marrying recently-met brides in a ceremony presided over by a priest who might well be as inebriated as the groom. Since there was no state involvement in the ceremony, all manner of ill-advised unions took place. However, this was not deemed to be a problem until the marriages became a bit more fashionable and began to spread upwards in society.

In fact, the Bill was opposed at the time in Parliament for being a way to close ranks against the lower classes since a public announcement of marriage between the classes would embarrass both parties.

Charles Townsend, speaking in Parliament, described it as 'one of the most cruel measures ever directed against the fairer sex'. "If I were ever concerned in promoting it I should expect to have my eyes torn out by the young women of the last country town I passed through, for against such an enemy I could not surely hope for the protection of the gentlemen of our army." Robert Nugent, also in Parliament, said: "It is certain that proclamation of banns and a public marriage is against the genius and nature of our people … it shocks the modesty of a young girl to have it proclaimed through the parish that she is going to be married and a young fellow does not like to be exposed so long before to the jeers of all his companions."

Despite the prophecies of doom by members of the Opposition that the Act would be a huge impediment to easy and free marriage and would no longer allow the common man to marry above his station, the Act was generally a success. The clergymen who feared losing out on the marriage trade continued marrying couples and, in fact, did better than ever. Commoners continued to marry rich heiresses, albeit in a more sanctioned way and once they were of age.

The only place where the Act did not have effect was in Scotland, a nation in love with the notion of marriage as being a matter between the intended and a priest without the interference of the state. There was little change from the time of handfastings, with the only difference being that Gretna Green now did a roaring trade in English marriages.

Sir Walter Scott sets down the Scottish attitude to handfasting in his historical novel *The Monastery* (1820): 'We Border men are more wary than your inland clowns of Fife and Lothian – no jump in the dark for us – no clenching the fetters around our wrists until we know how they will wear upon us – we take our wives, like our horses, upon trial. When we are handfasted, as we term it, we are man and wife for a year and a day– that space gone by each may choose another mate, or at their pleasure may call the priest to marry them for life – and this we call handfasting.'

The practice was put paid to by the Church, which would much rather have unhappy marriages than, what was in its eyes, fornication. By 1563 it was decreed that to be legal a marriage had to be solemnised by a priest and have the consent of the Church. Across the Atlantic in New England there was also a movement against immoral mingling and the Puritan Fathers made life very difficult for bachelors, in the hope of encouraging early marriage. Single men were fined £1 a week for living alone, unless this had been sanctioned by the local authority. The town authorities also had to be consulted before a householder could host a bachelor as a lodger.

These two illustrations by caricaturist James Gillray in 1805 show a harmonious scene in the one called 'Harmony before marriage' and a chaotic one in the one called 'Matrimonial harmonics'. (*Public domain*)

Given that there were heavy financial penalties for even flirting with maidens, and imprisonment for habitual offenders, the best course of action was to submit to marriage with a partner chosen by your elders.

Of course, despite plays and novels suggesting sentiments to the contrary, marrying in defiance of your family was not always the path to true love. The example of Lady Elizabeth Fox Strangways shows what can happen when you wilfully ignore the advice of your elders. Lady Elizabeth's father was not overly keen on her marrying William Davenport Talbot, a man from the right social class but alas with no great prospects or property of his own, but they married nevertheless on 17 April 1796. It turned out that Elizabeth was not even in love with her unsuitable choice. She told her father that she was 'entirely unblinded by the illusions of love' and had no 'romantic attachment', but didn't want to hurt her persistent suitor and so, eventually gaining her father's permission, she married him.

The marriage had an unhappy ending. William sickened soon after his son's birth, but Elizabeth nevertheless left him to travel to Wales and, when he died soon afterwards, she did not even travel back to her father's house to attend his funeral. By contrast, her sister Harriot agreed to marry James Frampton. He had a modest fortune but also the approval of her family and friends, one of whom commented: 'On the whole, all circumstances considered, it is a desirable match for Harriot. Here is love and prudence in unison: tranquil love, if such there be, *sans délire*, *sans craint*, *sans agitation* and, as Rousseau would perhaps say, *sans amour* – but enough, I trust, for happiness.' They remained married for forty-five years, with many commenting on the geniality of their situation.

The drama of young love is not necessarily a good indicator of lasting contentment. One imagines that Lydia and Wickham's marriage in *Pride and Prejudice* (1813) will not be a happy one. Once lust and flirtation is done with, the sobering effects of married life put all defects under a magnifying glass. In the same novel, it is revealed that Mr. Bennet

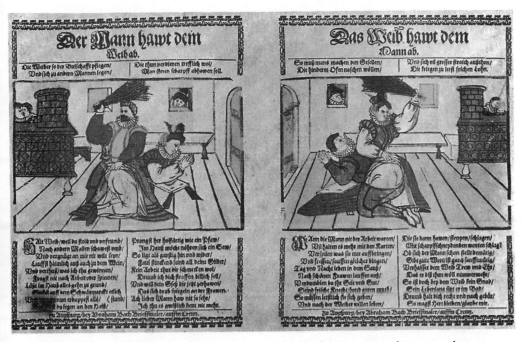

This woodcut by Abraham Bach, from the second half of the seventeenth century, shows a man beating his wife for being proud, impious, lazy and drunk while in the second scene she beats him for gambling, drinking, gluttony and chasing pretty girls. (*Public domain*)

married his wife for her looks and vivacity but soon discovered how ill matched they were.

Drunkenness was a defect that affected both men and women, as this woodcut by Abraham Bach shows. The gin craze of the early eighteenth century was the first time that women were allowed to drink alongside men. It is what led to gin getting its nickname of 'mother's ruin' and artist William Hogarth painted his famous Gin Lane at this time, depicting a mother dropping, in her alcoholic stupor, her child.

While this craze had a terrible effect on poorer couples, the rich had their own substance abuse issues. Opium, taken in the form of laudanum, was considered practically a cure-all and the concept of addiction to it was not a widely held belief. The Victorian love affair with laudanum meant that 280,000lbs of opium was being imported into Britain by 1860. Byron's only legitimate child, Ada, Countess of Lovelace (1815-1852), was addicted to opium – although it was probably more her infidelities that gave her husband pause for thought than her addiction. Laudanum was so widely used that even children were given

A painting by Edouard Henri Theophile Pingret shows a young couple visiting a savant. The suggestion is that the couple are asking whether their marriage would be propitious, or, if already married, when they would have children. c. 1833. (*Wellcome Library, London*)

a little drop of it if they were being too fractious for their mother's or nursemaid's liking.

A drugged up child, however, was better than no child; several marriages faltered due to childlessness. With none of the advanced fertility tests we have nowadays, it was a gamble as to whether that perfectly healthy-looking woman could produce a son and heir. For a man to take the 'blame' of being unable to father a child was a stretch too far and some men probably accepted the offspring of an affair for the twofold benefit of not appearing incapable of it themselves and denying that they had been cuckolded.

Divination and savants were one avenue that a couple could explore in the hope of discovering when, if ever, they would be with child, as Edouard Pingret's painting depicts. Divorce on the grounds of childlessness was a common occurrence when the lack of children could spell the end of a dynasty. Even Napoleon left his beloved Josephine for another woman when she couldn't give him an heir.

Vicious husbands

Domestic violence in marriage, while frowned upon in Victorian society, was not in any way a criminal matter. In fact, in 1857 the generally accepted law is the reported statement by a judge that a man may beat his wife as long as the rod he does it with is no thicker than his thumb – the rule of thumb. In 1895 a city of London byelaw was passed entitled Curfew on Wife Beating, which made hitting your wife between the hours of 10pm and 7am illegal in order to stop the noise keeping neighbours awake.

Another law governing violence in the home was the longstanding one of coverture; this held that a man and his wife and children became one legal entity for which he was responsible and therefore he could use physical or verbal abuse in the process of controlling them. Caroline Norton (1808–1877) used this law to her advantage in her dispute with her violent and possessive husband. When she left him, she used her

Engraving by John Cochran of Caroline Sheridan Norton, "the Honble. Mrs. Norton" (1808–1877). Undated. (*Harvard University*)

earnings as a writer to support herself, but George Norton successfully argued in court that he was entitled to her earnings as her husband. With nothing to live on, Caroline began to run up hefty debts and, when approached for payment, referred the creditors to her husband, forcing him to honour them.

Caroline was devastated at being parted from her children when she left George. He retained custody as was his legal right and refused to allow Caroline not just access to them but even information about where they were. He only relented after her youngest son had a fall and was gravely ill and likely to die; alas by the time Caroline was sent for, it was too late and her child was dead. After this George permitted her to see her other sons, but always under supervision.

This led her to tirelessly campaign for the rights of divorced and separated mothers to see their children. While no feminist, thanks to her work and that of other campaigners of the day, the Custody of Infants Act 1839, the Matrimonial Causes Act 1857 and the Married Women's Property Act 1870 were all passed. This last Act ensured that women retained the property they came into a marriage with rather than automatically having it transfer over to their husbands. This finally released women from coverture and ensured they had a greater chance to escape violent marriages. It is a sobering thought though that it would be 1976 before Britain had a piece of legislation dedicated to stamping out domestic violence – the Domestic Violence and Matrimonial Proceedings Act – and 1991 before marital rape was made illegal.

Lesbian lovers

There is an apocryphal tale that in the 1885 legislation re-criminalising male homosexuality, lesbianism was also due to become a crime, but Queen Victoria did not believe it existed in England, thinking instead it was some strange French perversion. Whether that is true or not, it is clear that the lack of legislature meant a degree of freedom for lesbians in their courtship that wasn't there for gay men. Although, regrettably, it also meant that the history of lesbianism is also sadly lacking.

An etching from 1820 entitled 'Love-a-la-mode or two dear friends' shows Lady Louisa Strachan and Lady Sarah Warwick enjoying an embrace while their husbands discuss what is to be done about the 'disgraceful business'. Some experts, such as Dr Lesley Hall, have said that this may not have had much to do with female sexuality at all since it may have been a jibe at Admiral Strachan and Lord Warwick, calling their masculinity into question if their wives found each other's company more stimulating than their own. Strachan, despite the gossip and rumours, became an Admiral of the White in 1821, a year after this etching appeared.

Lady Strachan and Lady Warwick making love in a park, while their husbands look on with disapproval. Coloured etching, c.1820. (*Wellcome Library, London*)

The better documented case of a woman turning away from her marriage into the arms of her lesbian lover is that of Mariana Belcombe – although perhaps a more accurate way of putting it would be that she moved away from the arms of her lesbian lover into matrimony for money since the marriage came later. And what a lover her companion was! Anne Lister (1791–1840) is now known as the 'first modern lesbian' though what that epitaph appears to mean is that she is the first to have a clear idea about her homosexuality and to have defined it as such. Her diaries have been described as the 'dead sea scrolls of lesbianism'. Meticulously kept, the wealthy landowner used a code on about a sixth of the four million word diaries to write about the more intimate details of her romantic life, as well as documenting her work and improvements to the home she inherited in 1826 from her uncle, Shibden Hall near Halifax in Yorkshire.

Anne and Mariana were school friends who became lovers; from her own diaries, it appears that Anne was a very proficient seducer, having many lovers over the course of her life. The diary entry from 29 January 1821 states her acknowledgement of her sexuality: 'I love and only love the fairer sex and thus, beloved by them in turn, my heart revolts from any other love than theirs.'

Anne was heartbroken when Mariana married Charles Lawton in 1816, but they resumed their affair shortly afterwards. Anne wrote that Mariana passed on a venereal disease to her from her husband. When she went to Paris to find a cure for the disease, she had a number of affairs that made her turn away from Mariana and look for someone who could commit to living with her as a wife. The neighbouring estate was owned by Ann Walker, a wealthy landowner and, in Lister's eyes, an equal. Anne Lister seduced Walker and the two even had a Church blessing for their union.

Charles Lawton appears to have turned a blind eye to his wife's affair with Anne Lister, but he was enraged at discovering that the two were eagerly awaiting his death (he was twenty years older than his wife) so that they could be free to live together. When Mariana eventually decided to leave Charles, it was too late as Anne had by then decided to be with Walker.

Happily ever after?

Marrying an older man for money was a common occurrence throughout history and the fear of these older men that they would be cuckolded is played upon in historical satirical drawings and cartoons. It seems

A c.1832 lithograph shows a portly, well-to-do physician leaving his house, while his wife cavorts in the window with a younger man. (*Wellcome Library, London*)

A husband wearily pampers his pregnant wife. Reproduction of a lithograph, 1838. (*Wellcome Library, London*) shocking that so many affairs came to light in centuries past, despite the Church's insistence on fidelity as part of the marriage vows. It seems as though parishioners were busy flirting and fumbling through sermons instead of listening to them.

The reason for marriage in the Catholic Church was very specifically stated in canon law: 'The matrimonial covenant, by which a man and a woman establish between themselves a partnership of the whole of life and which is ordered by its nature to the good of the spouses and the procreation and education of offspring, has been raised by Christ the Lord to the dignity of a sacrament between the baptized.'

Most other churches, while leaving much catechism behind, do not abandon the idea that marriage goes hand-in-hand with procreation. It is easy to imagine the societal pressure on couples to have children. If a couple managed to be faithful to one another, the next obstacle to a happy marriage was the ability to have children. Yet, the arrival of children didn't always spell marital bliss. Even today we speak of the upheaval that children represent in a marriage – in earlier times when it was a given that women of a certain class would not work, it must have been very isolating to have no public life and many men fled the disruptions of domestic life for their clubs and male spaces. For poorer classes, the very fact of another mouth to feed was enough of a strain.

It seems that in courtship, it is the journey rather than the destination that counts, and the most successful couples were those who continued the journey after the milestone of marriage. The men who would continue to bring home flowers and ribbons or take their wives to state fairs and exhibitions were the ones with the happiest spouses and therefore the happiest lives.

Conclusion

Happiness in relationships relies on many factors but a few good sense bits of advice from our ancestors is not to be sniffed at – a summary of the best of their advice.

The modern world is obsessed with love and romance. Think about the TV shows and films we watch and the books we read. We love being in love. The way we love can often be influenced by social mores without us ever knowing where these rituals and norms originate.

Think of a marriage proposal in modern life: the man will go down on one knee and propose to his girlfriend. Yet many won't know that this tradition originates in eleventh century ideas of courtly love, in which the lover is considered the vassal of the beloved, who is the lord. We send Valentine's cards without knowing that this is a fairly modern tradition originating in the commercial nous of industrialised Victorians. We present our beloved with flowers, never knowing there is a whole language in the blooms we choose.

Some believe the trials and tribulations of courting in the modern age have put paid to romance and they yearn for times past when they imagine courtship was better and more chivalrous. Yet, if we've learned anything, romance throughout the ages came about through couples who ignored the social norms of marrying for money or family alliances. It came about from the husbands who did not have affairs or sue their wives for 'criminal conversation' and the wives who did not bankrupt their husbands or leave them for a fancier man. That rings as true today as in times past – it is often said, even by modern psychologists and relationship therapists, that contempt is the death of love.

The first flowering of love is exciting; a time when everything about our beau is fascinating and enchanting. This can quickly lead to disillusionment if we find that our idea of our partner is not quite the same as the reality of him or her. In the past couples have had to deal with artifice in looks and personality and perhaps we still do. After all, with a profusion of reality TV shows, we all know in forensic detail what a boob job, lips with fillers or botoxed foreheads look like. And, just as in the past, we have those who mock those 'improvements' and those who swear by them.

Perhaps the biggest change between how we courted in the past and how we do so now is how free we are to interact with each other, even live together, before marriage. The lack of a strong church forcing us to consider marriage or a government taxing those who do not marry (although they do give a bit of cash to those who do marry as an incentive to do so!) also mean that we spend a great deal longer dating than marrying. Many complain that it was easier in an earlier, more idyllic time when you would have ritualised methods of meeting a potential spouse within your sphere. But we should not be too nostalgic about the past; venereal diseases, the lack of women's rights, the lack of gay rights and backward attitudes toward morality made the past a country too terrible to live in.

The beauty of love tokens, the humour in silly ideas about men and women and the sheer joyousness of archaic language are the aspects of courting in the past that we can safely enjoy without any need to hark back to history as a better time for those wanting to find love. Returning to the writer we began our journey with, Aristophanes believed that love is composed of a single soul inhabiting two bodies. It is probably better to say love is when you find a way to have your soul fall into step with another's. Courtship is discovering the rhythm your step must take.

Further Reading

Anonymous, *The Gentleman's Letter Writer* (Old House, 2012)

Beeton, Samuel Orchart, *Complete Etiquette for Ladies* (Old House, 2011)

Binney, Ruth, *The Illustrated Wise Words & Country Ways* (David & Charles, 2007)

Brander, Michael, *The Perfect Victorian Hero: The Life and Times of Sir Samuel White Baker* (Mainstream, 1982)

Brown, Pamela Allen, *Better a Shrew Than a Sheep: Women, Drama, and the Culture of Jest in Early Modern England* (Cornell University Press, 2003)

Bryson, Bill, *At Home* (Black Swan, 2011)

Charles, CH, *Love Letters of Great Men and Women: From the Eighteenth Century to the Present Day* (Kessinger, 1924)

Davis, Norman (edited by), *The Paston Letters* (Oxford University Press, 1983)

Douglas-Fairhurst, Robert (edited by), *A Selected Edition of London Labour & the London Poor by Henry Mayhew* (Oxford University Press, 2010)

Downing, Sarah Jane, *Beauty and Cosmetics 1550-1950* (Shire, 2012)

Farrar, Mrs John, *The Young Lady's Friend* (American Stationers Co, 1838)

Flanders, Judith, *The Victorian House* (Harper Perennial, 2004)

Fraser, Antonia, *The Weaker Vessel: Woman's Lot in Seventeenth-Century England* (Phoenix, 2002)

Gatrell, Vic, *The First Bohemians* (Allen Lane, 2013)

Hardy, Rev. EJ, *The Love Affairs of Some Famous Men* (T.Fisher Unwin, 1897)

Hartley, Cecil B, *The Gentleman's Book of Etiquette and Manual of Politeness* (DeWolfe, Fiske & Co, 1875)

Henderson, William, *Notes on the Folk Lore of the Northern Counties of England and the Borders 1866* (Longmans, Green & Co, 1866)

Hughes, Kathryn, *The Short Life & Long Times of Mrs Beeton* (Harper Perennial, 2006)

Leyser, Henrietta, *Medieval Women: A Social History of Women in England 450-1500* (Phoenix, 1996)

Lister, Anne, Edited by Helena Whitbread, *The Secret Diaries of Miss Anne Lister* (Virago, 2010)

Martin, Joanna, *Wives and Daughters: Women and Children in the Georgian Country House* (Hambledon Continuum, 2004)

Miles, Alice, *Every Girl's Duty: The Diary of a Victorian Debutante* (Andre Deutsch, 1992)

Newby, Jennifer, *Women's Lives: Researching Women's Social History 1800-1939* (Pen & Sword, 2011)

Ralls, Karen, *Medieval Mysteries: A Guide to History, Lore, Places and Symbolism* (Ibis, 2014)

Rubenhold, Hallie (edited by), *Harris's List of Covent Garden Ladies* (Transworld, 2012)

Summerscale, Kate, *Mrs Robinson's Disgrace* (Bloomsbury, 2013)

Turner, ES, *A History of Courting* (Michael Joseph, 1954)

Wilhelm, James J., *Lyrics of the Middle Ages: An Anthology* (Routledge, 1990)

Wilson, AN, *The Victorians* (Arrow, 2003)

Worsley, Lucy, *If Walls Could Talk: An Intimate History of the Home* (Faber & Faber, 2012)

Wright, Thomas, *The Homes of Other Days* (Trubner & Co, 1871)

Index